FERVENT SERVANT:
DIVINELY PREPARED TO COUNSEL

Navigating the Essentials
of Biblical Counseling

A BEST SELLING AUTHOR
DOUG CARRAGHER, TH.D.

Fervent Servant: Divinely Prepared to Counsel
Navigating the Essentials of Biblical Counseling

Copyright © 2024

Doug Carragher, Th.D.

This book is the intellectual property of Douglas J. Carragher, Th.D. All rights reserved. No part of this publication may be used or reproduced, stored in, or introduced into a retrieval system, or transmitted in any form or by any means (printed, written, photocopied, electronic, audio, or otherwise) without prior written permission of the author.

All Scripture quotations are from the King James Version of the Bible.

Cover design and layout: Brad Sherman

Acknowledgments

Above all, I would like to express my deepest gratitude to my Lord and Savior, Jesus, for saving my soul. My love and devotion to Him is unwavering. In addition, I want to express my gratitude for many others:

To my wife, Debbie, who has captured my heart and served as my rock throughout all these years: You are not only my best friend but also the mother of our children and my personal hero. Your love and unwavering support have illuminated my life, making it brighter and more meaningful. You're still the one!

To my children, Doug II, his dear wife Madeline, and Daniel, your love and encouragement mean the world to me. I am immensely grateful for your continued support and your presence in my life. I am very proud of you.

To the late First Sergeant Willie Vernon Watson: You pointed me to a Savior when my magnetic north was aimed at a career, money, prestige, and pride: I saw Christ in you. Your passing in my arms changed my trajectory toward love, service, an understanding of PTSD, and a journey of helping those affected by it. Your life mattered to me and to tens of thousands of others who have read my books.

To Chaplain Dennis Kennedy: You dedicated a lifetime ministering to the soldiers of the United States Army. Your unwavering commitment to sharing the gospel and embracing me as I grieved the loss of a friend, and subsequently, introducing me to the greatest Friend I will ever know, is deeply appreciated.

To Chaplain Bob Wido: Your unwavering support and dedication made an indelible impact on my life and Debbie's. Amid the most challenging circumstances, you stood as a beacon of strength and faith, guiding not only me but also my unsaved wife through trying times. Your exemplary personal integrity and unyielding determination placed you at the heart of our journey. I am profoundly grateful for the invaluable lessons we learned from you and for the profound role you played in leading my beloved wife, Debbie, to embrace the saving grace of Christ. Chaplain Bob, you are a true hero, and your presence in our lives is deeply cherished and esteemed by our entire family.

To the most impactful people in my life: Despite having broken hearts and painful bodies, you have experienced betrayal, rejection, and abandonment by those you loved the most. Yet, with shaky voices and wobbly knees, you surrendered to your Savior. It's incredible how the Lord has replaced your weaknesses with His strength and has transformed you for His glory. I can almost always spot you in any church because you may be weeping or laughing, but you're always wholly engaged. I'm always in awe of the Lord's work in your lives, and this book is my attempt to bring others to the Cross. The Lord always uses a surrendered believer's testimony for His glory. You all led by example and still touch my life.

Table of Contents

Foreword		1
Chapter 1	The Purpose of Biblical Counseling	11
	The Need For Biblical Counseling	*13*
	Eight Characteristics of An Effective Biblical Counselors	*15*
	What Biblical Counseling Is	*23*
	Fifteen Principles of Biblical Counseling	*26*
Chapter 2	Preparing for the Counseling Session	31
	Personal Preparation	*33*
	Examine Yourself	*38*
	Practical Preparation (logistical)	*45*
	Compile Data on the Counselee	*48*
	Comply with Mandatory Reporting Requirements	*52*
Chapter 3	Understanding Human Nature and Sin	57
	The Image of God	*61*
	The Fall of Humanity	*63*
	Humanity's Inherent Sinfulness	*64*
	Guilt and Consequences of Sin	*66*
	The Struggle with Sin	*67*
	Repentance and Forgiveness	*69*
	The Role of the Law	*70*
	Redemption through Christ	*71*
	Justification and Sanctification	*72*
	The Role of the Holy Spirit	*74*
	God's Grace and Mercy	*75*
	Identity in Christ	*76*
	Overcoming Shame and Regret	*77*
	Renewing the Mind	*79*
	Coping with Temptation	*80*
	Extending Grace to Others	*81*
	Healing from Past Wounds	*82*
	Living a Spirit Filled Life	*83*
	Cultivating Repentant Hearts	*85*
	Embracing the Journey of Redemption	*86*

Chapter 4	**Mistakes in Biblical Counseling**... 89
	Overreliance on Personal Opinions 92
	Lack of Cultural Sensitivity.. 94
	Judgmental Attitude 96
	Ignoring Underlying Mental Health Issues............................... 98
	Insufficient Knowledge of Scripture... 100
	Imposing Solutions... 101
	Ineffective Communication.. 103
	Emotional Overinvolvement.. 105
	Unrealistic Expectations 106
	Neglecting Self-Care... 108
Chapter 5	**Counseling Techniques and Skills** 111
	Active Listening.. 113
	Showing Compassion 115
	Reflecting... 116
	Asking Open-Ended Questions.. 118
	Offering Encouragement 119
	Dependence on God 121
	Sufficiency in Scripture Alone.. 123
	Providing a Safe Environment... 125
Chapter 6	**Master Plan for Conducting a Biblical** .... 127 **Counseling Session**
	Overview of the Master Plan.. 129
	Detailed Look at Each Step 131
	Seeking God's Guidance... 135
	Active Listening.. 137
	Identification of Root Issues 138
	Scriptural Application 139
	Prayerful Reflection 141
	Goal Setting.. 142
	Homework Assignments... 144
	Accountability 145
	Unresolved Questions... 147
	Encouragement and Hope 149
	Resources.. 151
	Conclusion of the Session 152
	Documentation 154
Chapter 7	**Self-Examination and Self-Care** 157
Chapter 8	**Mandatory Reporting**.. 163

Chapter 9	Clear and Direct Communication 167
Chapter 10	Recordkeeping 171
	What Records to Keep 173
	Benefits of Recordkeeping 175
	Guidelines for Recordkeeping 176
Appendix A	Helping Hurting People Understand the Biblical Need .... 179 for Military and First Responders to Kill
Appendix B	Replacing Sinful Behavior with Godly Behavior 187
Appendix C	Examples and Case Studies 201
Appendix D	Checklist for a Counseling Session 209
Appendix E	Pre-Counseling Questionnaire 211

FOREWORD

My Life Story in Brief

*I've come to understand that
there's nothing in this world
that can torment you as profoundly
as your own thoughts.*

My Life Story in Brief

My life includes its share of contradictions and trials. I entered this world as the sixth child of Francis and Jeanine (Girardin) Carragher. Tragically, my eldest sibling, a brother, met his fate at birth, thus uniting me with only four older siblings. Externally, our family presented an image of being normal and admirable. The outside world held the belief that my father was a benevolent, profoundly spiritual, and extraordinary man. As a World War II veteran, his public persona exuded charisma because of his towering stature, striking handsomeness, and physical fitness. He made deliberate efforts to engage with people, and his vitality illuminated any space he entered. When I was very young, I sometimes wondered whether he was the leader of the entire world.

Regrettably, the walls of our home concealed my father's dark persona—narcissistic, abusive, and ensnared by alcohol, often entangled with extramarital relationships. These early memories bear the weight of witnessing him inflict harm on my mother and my siblings, making tears our constant companions. A vivid recollection etched in my mind involves my courageous brother Francis. Only eight years old at the time, he fearlessly interposed himself between our mother and our father, who seemed to be possessed by a malevolent spirit, and attempted to shield her from the brutality. Francis's bravery endures as a heroic example to me. When I was just six, my father abandoned us, relocating to another state. Paradoxically, we found ourselves in a somewhat improved situation during his absence, and for several years, we had no idea where he was.

My father cunningly evaded his obligation of child support. Only when ordered by a court to fulfill his responsibility did he employ the excuse of financial destitution, begrudgingly dispatching a meager seventy-five dollars each month to support five children. Even by the standards of 1969, this amounted to less than 5 percent of his income. We struggled along with minimal financial resources and the lack of insurance. It was the assistance of welfare and state aid that extended a lifeline, eventually enabling us to break free from the clutches of destitution.

The subsequent years were defined by our poverty. Although these experiences were painful and occasionally humiliating, they imparted to us a serene form of love that I would not exchange for the world's treasures. During this period, my mother toiled at a mill on the overnight shift and also worked as a school bus driver during the day. Our old tattered clothing, along with our lack of grooming and social finesse, invited ridicule from other children. The presence of foster children in our home further fueled the taunting. Despite these social tribulations, we were graced with a love untouched by the specter of abuse, a gift whose worth we would never underestimate.

It seemed like Ray (Doten), my stepfather, came into our lives out of nowhere. He and my mother worked together at Royal Metal Mills in Plainfield, Connecticut. He must have been blinded by love or crazy to want to join and lead our tribe. He was ten years younger than my mother. When Ray came on the scene, there were no less than eight kids, including foster children, living with us. My mother invited him over several times, and it was clear they were in love. My mother, always the communicator, had conversations with Ray and us, emphasizing that we, the children, were her top priority and that there would be no changes in that. Ray would join our family only if we all agreed to their marriage. Their courtship was slow and intentional. They acted like grown-ups who were worthy of our respect, and I cannot stress how much that assurance helped our family. It proved that our mother and Ray were honorable, dependable, and chose us. Their love was unconditional, and they had a greater calling, which was their love for us. I never needed therapy for any decision they ever made. We needed their trauma-free love and dependability more than ever, and the Lord used them and their love to help us succeed. They were my heroes.

I remember that at first we were skeptical, indifferent, and outright afraid of Ray, because of the damage our father had done. A mental health professional could spend years studying our father, the trauma, and the collateral damage he brought to our lives. However, we soon realized that Ray was the opposite of our father, and we wanted him.

We encouraged the marriage. The feeling was unanimous. Ray did not have a pretentious or nefarious bone in his body. For decades he represented the stable leadership we needed in our world.

Our family dynamic was unique. We had foster kids, and my older sisters had boyfriends who were always hanging around. Our cars were old and cheap, which meant they frequently broke down. We knew we were what some people would call "poor hillbillies." However, what we did have was respect and love for each other. Even amid the craziness of merging families and lives, we looked out for one another.

Ray brought his son, Scott, into our family. We had Scott with us every weekend and for a month during the summers. Even though Ray made less than my father did, he paid more in child support for one child than my father paid for five kids. Although Ray worked hard as a mill worker, his wages were low, but he became an example that every family should have. Working twelve hours a day five days a week, he exemplified steadiness. He was "all in" for our family.

School for me is a blur; it was a necessary but uninspiring part of my life. I missed out on many blessings and was eventually expelled for smoking marijuana. It would have been easy for me to fall through the cracks and fail in life, but my mother and Ray wouldn't allow it. They constantly reassured me that I could succeed, that I was smart, and that I had simply made mistakes. They taught me that people mess up, but one's character is defined by how he recovers. They believed in my recovery, and their unwavering support made them great cheerleaders in my life.

In 1978, I believed I had discovered my path to complete recovery when, at seventeen years and one day old, I enlisted in the army with my mother's consent. Just five days later, I departed for basic combat training at Fort Leonard Wood, Missouri. My father expressed his sentiments through a letter in which he asserted that I was a failure and would perpetually remain one. As had been the case for most of his life, he opted for abuse and condemnation, but he was ultimately proven wrong. For that, my profound gratitude extends to the God I serve because He rewrites lives and provides illumination even in the darkest of circumstances. While there will always be naysayers with their hurtful opinions, it's crucial to follow the path of Christ, for therein lies our salvation.

During my military career, I had the privilege of crossing paths with Deborah Sue Andrews, and she completely transformed my world. Her sense of humor, unwavering optimism, and shared conservative outlook on life resonated deeply with me. In just a year, we became a couple, got engaged, and eventually embarked on what is now a forty-one-year journey of marriage. Her influence has extended into every corner of my life, leaving no facet untouched.

What stands out as a remarkable testament to our faith journey is that nine months after I embraced my Lord and Savior, Debbie followed suit. Her acceptance of Him was a profound blessing in our lives, and I am extremely grateful to the Lord for bringing her into my life.

My service in the army exposed me to many traumatic situations, several so intense that they were etched in my identity. As a young noncommissioned officer, I witnessed a soldier drive a piece of heavy equipment over the side of a bridge into a small river. The equipment flipped over and trapped the soldier underwater. I tried unsuccessfully to administer underwater mouth-to-mouth resuscitation, coming up for breaths of life in between, but Private First-Class Francis Mackie tragically lost his life that day. The memory remains vivid in my mind, along with the scent of late spring air.

My army career is a testament to how all those who join the service start at the same level and must prove their worth. I was provided with educational opportunities and promotions, and I excelled in various soldier competitions. I found an avenue to succeed where I wasn't considered odd or different, and I was given opportunities for higher education and training. I seized almost every opportunity that came my way. I entered the army needing a single credit to officially graduate from high school, but I left with four college degrees. I never forgot where I came from and felt a special connection with the unique soldiers I encountered. The Lord used my journey in the army to grow me as a Christian leader.

Nine years in, while serving as a leader in the Quick Reaction Force at Fort Harrison, Indiana, my fellow soldiers and I responded to a devastating plane crash. An Air Force jet had tragically crashed into a hotel lobby in Indianapolis, resulting in the loss of nine lives and injuries to others. Initially assigned to guard sensitive equipment, we were later tasked with the solemn duty of helping to recover the bodies of the nine victims. Each face or what remained of it is an indelible, haunting image etched into my mind. I am thankful the Lord has tempered the memories.

The event that would profoundly shape the narrative and every book I have written occurred on October 15, 1993. Following an intense army physical training session, my best friend, First Sergeant Willie Vernon Watson, suddenly collapsed. Without hesitation, I began to administer cardiopulmonary resuscitation (CPR), a procedure that involved both chest compressions and the breath of life. With each breath, I vividly recall blood spurting from a cut on Willie's lip into my mouth. Tragically, despite my best efforts, Willie did not survive. We later learned that his untimely passing was due to a heart defect that caused his left ventricular artery to detach from his heart. He was gone before he even hit the ground.

Willie, a devout born-again Christian, served as a profound example of faith and conservative values throughout his lifetime. His unwavering dedication to his beliefs left an indelible mark on my heart. After his death, his influence played a significant role in my decision to accept the Lord Jesus Christ as my personal Savior. Following Willie's memorial service, Chaplain Kennedy shared the gospel from the Bible and guided me toward the essential truths required for me to accept the Lord. I was saved on October 15, 1993, a transformative moment that further shaped my Christian and conservative convictions.

Sadly, the haunting memories of Willie's death continued to torment me for years, subjecting me to a relentless cycle of reliving those traumatic events. The specter of post-traumatic stress disorder (PTSD) loomed large, with the crushing weight of survivor's guilt bearing down on my soul. However, it was during those darkest hours that I found my salvation in faith, ultimately accepting Jesus as my Lord and Savior. That was the point in my life where the healing began.

I began to wholeheartedly immerse myself in the teachings of the Bible by attending Bible college and seminary, seeking solace and guidance from its profound wisdom. My newfound faith became the driving force in my life, propelling me to pursue higher education and spiritual understanding. I embarked on a journey of academic and spiritual growth, which culminated in the attainment of four graduate degrees, including a master's degree in theology, a master's degree in religious education and biblical counseling, and as the pinnacle of my academic achievement, a doctorate in theology.

Armed with the knowledge and spiritual insight gained from my extensive education, I embarked on a path marked by unwavering faith, seven years of fervent prayer, and dedicated study. It was through this transformative process that I finally discovered the help and inner peace I had so desperately prayed for. Inspired by the remarkable power of God's faithfulness and patience, I felt compelled to share the healing journey I had undergone with my fellow believers who were still searching for answers.

The result of this continued journey was my first book, *Wounded Spirits: A Biblical Approach to Post-Traumatic Stress*. Its publication opened doors and introduced me to individuals I would have never imagined meeting. Our bonds transcended mere friendship; they became akin to family, rooted in a profound respect for our shared faith. It's a testament to the power of God's grace. I discovered that the most unreached and unhealed segment of our population is the millions who are living with profound emotional wounds. Each day, I am committed to extending my hand to help them heal. I've taken on the role of an educator, produced a television show, and launched a daily podcast titled "Help for Wounded Spirits."

In all of this, I have found my life's true calling and work. My personal journey of healing from PTSD evolved into a mission to help others find their own paths to recovery and to teach leaders how to biblically counsel people with trauma—all to bring honor and glory to my Lord and Savior. I am deeply grateful to the Lord for His blessings and guidance along this transformative journey. My PTSD, once a source of profound pain, has become a source of strength, and the Lord is using it to bring glory to His name. I no longer relive the hurtful events that caused my PTSD, but I do remember the original pain and how the Lord's grace has changed my hurt; and weaknesses to His strengths and our successes. Essentially, I no longer relive the hurt, I remember the journey of grace and seek to help others find their mission.

Through these pages I will introduce you to Bible truths for effective biblical counseling.

CHAPTER 1

The Purpose of Biblical Counseling

In biblical counseling, we recognize that God is the ultimate Counselor, and His Word serves as the ultimate guide for how we should live our lives.

The Need for Biblical Counseling

Life is messy, complicated, and filled with ups and downs that can be very painful. It wasn't supposed to be this way. The Lord created a perfect world. The biblical Garden of Eden, also called the Garden of God or Paradise, was a beautiful place of lush vegetation, fruit trees, blooming plants, and rivers. In the garden were two unique trees existed: the tree of life and the tree of the knowledge of good and evil. Man was to live by the tree of life, but he was not to touch the other tree, or he would die. God put Adam and Eve in charge of tending and keeping the garden with these instructions: "The LORD God commanded the man, saying, Of every tree of the garden thou mayest freely eat: But of the tree of the knowledge of good and evil, thou shalt not eat of it: for in the day that thou eatest thereof thou shalt surely die" (Gen 2:16–17).

Genesis 2:24–25 records that Adam and Eve became one flesh, suggesting that they enjoyed a God-ordained biblical monogamous physical relationship in the garden. Their lives were innocent and free from sin; they lived naked and unashamed. They were comfortable with their physical bodies and their passion. Living in perfect harmony with the Lord was a carefree harmony and love we will only know in heaven.

In the next chapter 3 of the book of Genesis, the perfect honeymoon took an unfortunate turn toward disaster when Satan, the serpent, arrived unannounced. The supreme liar and deceiver, he convinced Eve that God was holding out on them by forbidding them to eat of the fruit of the tree of the knowledge of good and evil. One of the weapons in Satan's arsenal is planting seeds of doubt, and Eve was seduced. She ate the fruit and gave some to Adam, who ate it too.

Though Eve was deceived by Satan, Adam knew exactly what he was doing when he ate, and he did it anyway. Both sinned. Both rebelled against God's instructions. Their carefree harmony was gone.

Chapter 1

Suddenly everything changed! The couple's eyes were opened to a new evil reality. They felt ashamed of their nakedness and looked for a way to cover themselves. For the first time, they hid from God in fear.

God could have destroyed them, but instead, He lovingly reached out to them. When He asked them about their transgressions, Adam blamed Eve and Eve blamed the serpent. Responding in a typically human way, neither was willing to accept responsibility for their sin. Every day I deal with people who like Adam and Eve refuse to take responsibility for their sin.

God, in His righteousness, pronounced judgment, first on Satan, then on Eve, and finally on Adam. Then God, in His profound love and mercy, covered Adam and Eve with garments made from animal skins. This was a foreshowing of animal sacrifices that would be instituted under the law of Moses for the atonement of sin. Ultimately, this act pointed to the perfect sacrifice of Jesus Christ, which covered the sin of man once and for all.

Adam and Eve's disobedience in the Garden of Eden is known as the "fall of man." As a result of that fall, the Garden of Eden was lost to them:

> And the LORD God said, Behold, the man is become as one of us, to know good and evil: and now, lest he put forth his hand, and take also of the tree of life, and eat, and live for ever: Therefore the Lord God sent him forth from the garden of Eden, to till the ground from whence he was taken. So he drove out the man; and he placed at the east of the garden of Eden Cherubims, and a flaming sword which turned every way, to keep the way of the tree of life. (Gen 3:22-24)

Because Adam and Eve had eaten the fruit of the tree of knowledge of good and evil, the Lord sent them out of the Garden of Eden into the world. Their physical condition changed because of their eating of the forbidden fruit. As God had promised, they became mortal. They and their children would experience sickness, pain, and physical death. All these things hurt people and left them needing counseling.

Because of their transgression, Adam and Eve also suffered spiritual death. This meant they and their children could not walk and talk face to face with God. Adam and Eve and their children were separated from God both physically and spiritually. They needed sacrifices to atone for their sin. Today, we still need sacrifices to atone for our sin. Thankfully, we have a Savior who is the ultimate sacrifice and payment for our sins.

The single most important thing counselors must do is to ensure that their counselees have accepted Christ as their Lord and Savior. Once a counselee accepts Jesus, he or she is indwelled by the Holy Spirit and can now receive the biblical illumination necessary to understand the biblical counselor's instruction, which can lead to healing.

Eight Characteristics of Effective Biblical Counselors

One of the questions that I am asked regularly is "Aside from biblical qualifications, what characteristics should people look for in a biblical counselor?" This short list is my answer:

1. Counselors must be genuine believers, not Christians in name only. Here are a few of the things that means:

    - **They have had their previous sins forgiven.** They accept that everything wrong they have ever done has been removed from their permanent record. God will no longer count it against them. All debts are completely forgiven (1 John 1:9).

    - **They're justified before God.** *Justified* is a legal term that means one has been declared righteous in God's sight. Someone might ask, "How can God *justify* letting sinners into heaven?" The answer is that because of what Christ has done, our faults are not counted against us, and therefore God's acceptance of us is justified. We enjoy right standing with God (Rom 5:1).

- **They're adopted into God's family.** God is Father only to those who are brought into His family. Everyone who repents and has saving faith in Christ enjoys this status, being adopted into the family of God as a beloved son or daughter. If that's true of you, your Father is the King of the universe! (John 1:12).

"In today's society, the term adoption is the legal process by which an individual or couple becomes the legal parents of a child who is not their biological offspring. This process involves transferring all parental rights and responsibilities from the biological parents (or the state, in some cases) to the adoptive parents. Adoption can provide a child with a permanent family and is often pursued by individuals or couples who wish to expand their families or provide a home to a child in need."[1]

Understanding adoption in the New Testament we must look at and analyze Galatians chapter 4 verses 1-7. Galatians reads: *"Now I say, That the heir, as long as he is a child, differeth nothing from a servant, though he be lord of all; But is under tutors and governors until the time appointed of the father. Even so we, when we were children, were in bondage under the elements of the world: But when the fulness of the time was come, God sent forth his Son, made of a woman, made under the law, To redeem them that were under the law, that we might receive the adoption of sons. And because ye are sons, God hath sent forth the Spirit of his Son into your hearts, crying, Abba, Father. Wherefore thou art no more a servant, but a son; and if a son, then an heir of God through Christ."*

Paul is giving an analogy to the Galatians, using a child who is an heir. When this child matures, his father will give him an inheritance, making him the owner of everything. However, as long as the heir is a child, he is no different from a slave. The child lacks the responsibility and authority of an owner. In terms of responsibility and freedom, both the child and the slave are equal. Despite being the inheritor of his father's estate, the child does not yet possess the authority that comes with the inheritance.[2]

While still a child, the heir has guardians and managers making decisions for him and teaching him maturity until it's time for his father to grant him authority over the inheritance. Paul says that in the fullness of time, God sent forth His Son, Jesus. Jesus was born of a woman and born under the Law, likely referring to the children of Israel who were under the Law. This fits the context since Paul's letter primarily contests against Jewish authorities trying to convert believing Galatian Gentiles to live under Jewish Law.[3]

Jews, like Jesus, born under the Law, can now be redeemed from it through Jesus. They no longer have to be like children or slaves, answering to managers. They can now receive the adoption as sons. In Roman culture, children went through two phases of transitioning into adulthood and receiving the inheritance of helping run the family. This process was called "adoption," or more specifically "son-placing." Son-placing referred to the formal process where a child was recognized and established as an heir with the full rights and responsibilities of a son. It did not mean joining a new family but rather ascending to a place of authority within the family. The first phase of son-placing was at age 14, granting voting rights. The second phase was at age 25, granting property rights and the authority to make decisions as an owner.[4]

Jesus freed the Jews from being like children or slaves under a master—the Law. Instead of being dictated by the Law, they are now sons and have the authority to decide on their own.

Chapter 1

If Jesus freed Jews from the Law, it would not make sense for Gentiles who believe in Jesus to come under the Law.

Paul includes the Gentile Galatians in the analogy. Gentiles were also like children before Jesus, but unlike Jews, who were under the Law, Gentiles were held in bondage under the elemental things of the world. Though not under the Law, Jews are included as being under the elemental things of the world when Paul says "we," including himself under the sin of the world. Everyone begins as part of the world, which has its own rules. To "get ahead," the world demands specific behavior, including pagan religious worship for the Galatians.[5]

When the fullness of time came, God sent Jesus for both Gentiles and Jews. Just as Jesus made Jews sons, He made Gentiles sons. The Galatians, like the Jews, are no longer like children or slaves but are sons with the freedom and responsibility of adults, possessing the authority to decide for themselves.

The fullness of time refers to the perfect timing of Christ's coming. The Roman Empire ruled the Middle East, making travel easier with its roads; Greek was the common language; there were no major wars due to Roman governance; and the Jews, under Roman occupation, were ready for a Messiah to restore the Kingdom to Israel. These conditions made it the perfect time for Jesus to come and for the Gospel to spread after His return to Heaven.

God chose this period, the fullness of time, to send His Son, born of a woman and under the Law, emphasizing Jesus's humanity and Jewish upbringing under the Old Testament Law. He came to redeem those under the Law so they might receive the adoption as sons.

The Galatians know they are sons because of the Spirit. Paul says that because Jesus came, we have the Spirit of His Son in our hearts. Gentiles no longer need to follow the world's rules as slaves. They have been adopted as sons. The Spirit of His Son leads them to follow God, crying Abba, Father! Abba is a term of familiarity, like calling God "Daddy." This is the believers' connection to God.

Therefore, Paul writes, the Galatians are no longer slaves but sons; if sons, then heirs through God. We are sons and heirs to God because of Jesus Christ, and the Spirit within us calls out to the Father. This inner testimony of the Spirit assures us of our adoption as sons.

Ultimately, the New Testament word for adoption means to place as an adult son, often referred to as "son-placing." It has to do with our standing in the family of God. We are not little children but adults with all the privileges of sonship.[6]

- **They have passed from darkness to light.** In this world, two kingdoms are at war: the kingdom of darkness and the kingdom of light. When we are born again, we pass from being under the rulership of the devil to being under the rulership of Christ. We are rescued from the domain of Satan and become partakers in God's kingdom (Col 1:13).

- **Their hearts are indwelled by the Holy Spirit**, who lives within all believers, granting them faith and the power to live a new life. This is evidenced by the fruit of the Spirit, as God's work in our lives gradually makes us more Christlike (Eph 1:13).

- **They have inherited eternal life.** We usually think of eternal life as something we will experience later, but the Bible teaches that we receive eternal life at the moment of conversion. Every time the eternal life of Christians is mentioned in Scripture, it is in the present tense—meaning it is a current reality, not merely a future one. Though our bodies will die, our spirits are alive forever and later will be reunited with our resurrected physical bodies (John 3:36).

- **They are no longer under God's wrath.** As sinners, all people are under God's just wrath. He is angry over our sin, and it offends Him greatly. But through our faith in Christ, we move out from under God's wrath to being under his eternal blessing. God is now forever and always for us, not against us (John 3:36).

- **They're given Christ's righteousness.** Not only are our sins forgiven, but we are also given the righteousness of Christ. This means that the perfect, sinless life of Jesus is credited to our account. This has been called by some the "great exchange" because we give God our worst and in response are given His best (2 Cor 5:21).

- **They've been granted a place in God's kingdom.** Though we were shut out from God's kingdom and presence because of our sin and rebellion, through faith in Christ we can be welcomed back into it. They will forever be in God's presence, participating in kingdom life with all of the redeemed (Matt 25:34).

- **Their eyes have been opened to the beauty of God.** When we're unbelievers, sin clouds our vision. Because of this, we see sin and think it looks wonderful, and in turn see God and think He looks boring. When we are born again, however, the eyes of our hearts are opened, and we begin to see God for who He really is—our Creator, Father, Savior, and Treasure (2 Cor 4:3–6).

- **Their sin nature is defeated.** Without God's intervention, sin rules over us. We are slaves to its desires, unable to walk in holiness or please God at all. But through the new birth, we are new creations in Christ, and the rule of sin in our hearts is broken. Though we will continue to sin until we die and are glorified, the controlling power of sin is defeated, and we can overcome it through the help the Spirit provides (Rom 6:11).

- **Their salvation is guaranteed.** It would be a worrisome thing indeed if all of this were given to us but could, through some fault of our own, slip through our fingers and be lost. But the good news is that not only are all these blessings bought for us by the blood of Christ, but they are also secured for us by the blood of Christ. No one who belongs to Jesus will ever be cast away by Him. He will ensure that our faith endures to the end (Phil 1:6).

2. *They need to be good listeners and note takers.* Communication is a two-part process. It takes a speaker and a listener. Both are essential to good communication. As a counselor, if you do not listen well to the people you counsel, you're not doing your job. Next to God, they know themselves and their situations better than anyone else. Listening allows you to ask the right questions to help people dig deeper into their situation and see a broader biblical perspective. Listening helps you understand the people you counsel. Plus, when you listen well and take notes, it sets an example for them to listen well (and take notes), first to the Holy Spirit and then to you as their counselor (James 1:19).

3. *They need to have a thorough knowledge of Scripture.* Every biblical counselor is one who has studied the Word of God, has been taught the Word of God, and is continuing to grow in knowledge of the Word of God. This certainly includes ongoing Bible study, memorization, and training in biblical counseling. Biblical counselors must not only have their own daily time in Scripture for their own spiritual growth, but they must also pursue continued training in understanding and applying the Word of God.

4. *They need to have knowledge of the core truths of the Christian faith as well as the practical doctrines related to living the Christian life.* If we are going to instruct others in living the Christian life, then we must have knowledge of how to do so. However, none of us can fully

understand the Word of God. Finite human beings are incapable of perfectly understanding an infinite God, and so we cannot perfectly understand the inerrant Word of God that originated from God. Therefore, we must continue to study the Word of God and be filled with all knowledge.

5. *They need to be sympathetic.* I will never go through the same things that the people I see go through. I will never experience their hurt or pain. All of these are unique to them and their marriages. Yet, I can compassionately try to put myself in their shoes to see things from their perspective. I want them to know that I care about them. Even if I see several people each day in my office, I want each person or couple to feel as if he or she is the only one I am seeing that day.

6. *They need to put God first in their lives.* This is probably the most important thing for a counselor to do. When I as a counselor put God first, it clears away all the distractions that keep me from being the counselor God wants me to be. It creates a connection with God that gives me insight, wisdom, and answers that I would never have without Him. It's a choice: Should I operate each day as a counselor out of my own power or God's power? It's a no-brainer. God's power, hands down!

7. *If married, they need to have good marriages.* My experience tells me that the best marriage counselors are those who have good marriages. The marriage doesn't have to be perfect, but counselors who have been married a number of years have a long string of marital experiences. They have seen problems and issues and many of the negative things that can hit a marriage. They have seen God bring healing and growth, one problem and one issue at a time. For Debbie and me, God has used our marriage to grow us closer to each other and to Him. I would not be the counselor I am today without our marriage. I believe only married or widowed counselors should engage in marital counseling.

8. Most importantly, *biblical counselors must remember that the Lord is present in every counseling session*, guiding and blessing the process through prayer. The Lord is indeed an active participant in each session, at least as the third person present.

What Biblical Counseling Is

Bob Kellemen, academic dean and professor of biblical counseling at Faith Bible Seminary in Lafayette, Indiana, writes,

> Biblical counseling is Christ-centered, church-based, comprehensive, compassionate, and culturally-informed one another ministry that depends upon the Holy Spirit to relate God's Word to suffering and sin by speaking and living God's truth in love to equip people to love God and one another (Matt 22:35–40). It cultivates conformity to Christ and communion with Christ and the Body of Christ leading to a community of one-another disciple-makers (Matt 28:18–20).[7]

Biblical counseling is often misunderstood because it focuses on basic principles that are different from those underlying traditional counseling. With an emphasis on the care of the whole person—body, soul, and spirit—it relies on the values taught in the Bible. The goal of biblical counseling is to help people gain a sense of hope for their lives that is found in Jesus Christ. Biblical counselors use the discipline of theology as their foundation. Scripture is so central to the counseling process that a counselee may leave a session thinking that the use of the Bible is the only component.

A seasoned biblical counselor introduces Scripture and its teachings to help guide counselees through tough issues. Most counselees will seek to strengthen their faith during a time of struggle leading them to reach out to a biblical counselor.

In the midst of pain, people are searching for answers to life's questions, such as why they are suffering and what the meaning of their lives is. Biblical counseling will focus on helping clients achieve a better understanding of themselves and their relationship to God, while using counseling concepts to overcome anxiety, depression, grief, problems in their relationships, and past/present trauma.

Ultimately, biblical counseling is a process of discipleship that is laser-focused on the application of God's Word and walking in God's Spirit when dealing with matters of life.

The form and flow of biblical counseling does not have to be strictly defined. Biblical counseling may occur in a single moment or among believers following a Bible study or after a church service in the parking lot. Biblical counseling may happen between two people on a park bench or in a schoolteacher's classroom or in a pastor's office. The foundation of God's Word and the completed work of Jesus is the only absolute.

Biblical counseling may happen as a single event, but it is most effective and best understood as a series of events; that is, as a process. The process of encouraging sanctification, bearing with the suffering of others, and carefully applying the truth of God's Word in a hermeneutically correct way takes time. It takes time and study to believe and follow the gospel more fully each day. The grace of God, the power of His Spirit, and faithful human effort and study are needed during the process. It is not a last-minute session, but one that that the Lord can use the full counsel of His Word, and everything the counselor has experienced in his or her life for God's glory.

Therefore, for the counsel to be biblical it must follow four precepts. It must be rooted in God, exalting of Jesus Christ, enabled by the Holy Spirit, and offered in love.

- The precept of being "rooted in God" means that biblical counseling gets its motivations, hopes, content, methods, and power from God and according to His Word. For biblical counseling to be rooted in God, it must acknowledge God as the Creator of all things; uphold the sovereignty and authority of God; remain confident in God's eternal work in His people; rely on God's Word for knowledge, wisdom, and direction; embrace characteristics of God's counsel including love, hope, compassion, patience, wisdom, and mercy; and be devoted to God's glory.

- The precept of "exalting Jesus Christ" means that the gospel changes human hearts in a gloriously inexplicable way. Since the gospel is the essential message of biblical counseling, our counsel must uphold the deity of Christ, His incarnation, the sufficiency of His wrath-bearing death, His resurrection, His future return, His present and future kingdom, and His judgment of the world, among many other truths. We must ask the question, "Does my counsel present Jesus Christ as the one mediator between God and man and the person toward whom my sanctification is focused?" There is no other way, no other road, no other person leading to glory, peace, joy, love, unity, humility, purity of heart, clarity of conscience, and hope. Any promise of good and eternal change apart from (or in addition to) Christ is a false gospel that provides no hope.

- Power for a biblical counselor is found in the precept of being "'enabled by the Holy Spirit." We live to serve God's Holy Spirit, not the other way around. In other words, we don't use Him to serve our purposes; He uses us to serve His purposes. We are His ministers of grace. More than simply mentioning to the Holy Spirit, we actively trust the Holy Spirit to enable our counsel, to give understanding to the minds of the counselees, and to soften and transform their hearts. Every good and lasting change in the souls of people comes by the Spirit's power. We will delve deeper into allowing the Holy Spirit to work in our hearts in another chapter.

- The apostle Paul, writing to the church in Corinth, says that among the best ways to serve our fellow believers are the attributes of faith, hope, and love. He then states that the greatest of them is love. The precept of our counseling being "offered in love'" means that the relationship between the counselor and the counselee should be filled with and shaped by biblical love (1 John 4:7, Col 1:28–29). To be shaped by biblical love means to be motivated by affection for God and His genuine compassion for others. It means we seek whatever good the Lord gives a person or people we counsel. We should be less interested in the approval of people and more interested in their spiritual health. We should be less concerned about receiving praise from those we serve and more concerned about helping them give glory to the Lord Jesus Christ (John 3:26–30). Of course, faithfully holding to these principles will be dependent on the spiritual condition of our souls: "A good man out of the good treasure of his heart bringeth forth that which is good; and an evil man out of the evil treasure of his heart bringeth forth that which is evil: for of the abundance of the heart his mouth speaketh" (Luke 6:45)

As believers and biblical counselors, we seek the Lord for His grace in these areas, asking that He would help us know Him and His Word humbly and rightly and that we would learn to counsel according to the Word of the Lord, full of patience and the other fruits of the Spirit (Gal 5:22–26). We pray that we won't try to fix people and their problems but will love them well, counsel them with wisdom, and help them see and trust our Savior Jesus Christ. On my own, I can convince a person to change for, at best, a day or two; the Lord affects eternal change through conviction.

Fifteen principles of biblical counseling

1. Scripture as the foundation: The Bible is the authoritative and sufficient source of wisdom, truth, and guidance in biblical counseling. All counsel and interventions are based on God's Word.

2. God-centered approach: Biblical counseling centers on God as the ultimate Counselor and relies on His divine wisdom and power to bring about transformation in individuals' lives.

3. The gospel of grace: The message of salvation through Jesus Christ's atoning work is at the core of biblical counseling. Understanding and applying the gospel is vital for spiritual healing and growth.

4. Holy Spirit dependency: Recognizing the Holy Spirit's role as the Helper and Comforter, biblical counselors seek His guidance and empowerment in their counseling interactions.

5. Heart transformation: Biblical counseling targets the heart, addressing the inner attitudes, beliefs, and motives that drive behavior, leading to lasting change.

6. Repentance and forgiveness: Encouraging repentance for sin and extending forgiveness align with biblical principles, fostering restoration and reconciliation.

7. Love and compassion: Demonstrating Christlike love and compassion toward counselees creates an atmosphere of trust and safety, facilitating openness and healing.

8. Practical application: Rooted in Scripture, biblical counseling provides practical tools and strategies for applying biblical principles to daily life.

9. Personal responsibility: Encouraging counselees to take responsibility for their actions and decisions promotes accountability and growth.

10. Holistic approach: Biblical counseling addresses emotional, spiritual, relational, and physical aspects of individuals, recognizing their interconnectedness.

11. Prayerful guidance: Seeking God's direction and wisdom through prayer is an integral part of biblical counseling sessions.

12. Cultural sensitivity: While grounded in biblical truth, biblical counseling respects cultural diversity and applies God's Word to each person's unique context.

13. Discipleship and growth: Biblical counseling aims to equip and disciple individuals to walk in obedience to God and grow in their faith.

14. Humility and grace: Biblical counselors approach counselees with humility, acknowledging their own limitations and relying on God's grace throughout the counseling process.

15. Collaboration with the local church: Biblical counseling seeks to work in harmony with the local church community, fostering a holistic approach to spiritual care and support.

By adhering to these principles, biblical counseling provides a Christ-centered, transformative, and compassionate approach to addressing life's challenges and promoting spiritual growth and healing.

Chapter Summary

Key takeaways from Chapter 1 include the following:

- The importance of the Christian counselor being regenerate and being rooted in the forgiveness, justification, adoption, and other blessings provided through faith in Christ

- Characteristics of a good biblical counselor, including being a good listener, having a thorough knowledge of Scripture, being empathetic, and prioritizing God in one's life (Biblical counselors must remember that the Lord is present in every counseling session, guiding and blessing the process through prayer. The Lord is indeed an active participant in each session, at least as the third person present.)

- The definition and components of biblical counseling, emphasizing its Christ-centered, comprehensive, compassionate, and culturally informed nature

- Principles to follow in biblical counseling, such as Scripture as the foundation, a God-centered approach, reliance on the gospel, and a holistic view of individuals

This chapter stresses the centrality of God's Word and the gospel in counseling, the need for dependence on the Holy Spirit, and the importance of love, humility, and grace in counseling relationships.

---

[1] ChatGPT, response to "What does the term adoption mean?" July 17, 2024.

[2] Warren W. Wiersbe, "The Bible Exposition Commentary" Victor-Cook Communications Ministries, Colorado Springs, CO (2001) 705

[3] Kenneth S. Wuest, "Wuest Word Studies From the Greek New Testament" Wm. B. Eerdmans, Grand Rapids, MI (1950): 113

[4] Lehman Strauss, "Devotional Studies in Galatians and Ephesians", Loizeaux Brothers, Neptune, NJ (1957): 116.

[5] John Eadie, Commentary on the Epistle of Paul to the Galatians-based on the Greek Text, T. and T. Clark, Edinburgh, Scotland (1884): 299

[6] Warren W. Wiersbe, "The Bible Exposition Commentary" Victor-Cook Communications Ministries, Colorado Springs, CO (2001) 705

[7] Bob Kellemen, quoted in Journey to Biblical Counseling: An Interview with Bob Kellemen, https://counselingoneanother.com/2012/12/07/journey-to-biblical-counseling-an-interview-with-bob-kellemen/ 12/7/2012

Do you understand everything you have read in this chapter?
If not, please read it again before moving on to Chapter 2.

CHAPTER 2

Preparing for the Counseling Session

> *Biblical counseling goes beyond fixing issues; it's like being a spiritual mentor, helping people grow and become more like Christ.*

This chapter introduces the two main areas requiring a counselor's attention as you prepare to begin the counseling process: personal preparation (spiritual) and practical preparation (logistical). We will consider in detail several points in each category.

Personal Preparation

Pray with an understanding of the role of the Holy Spirit

The first thing to do once you know you will be meeting with a counselee is to pray. Regardless of how trivial or obvious this instruction may seem, you must realize that it is essential. The Lord reminds us, "Be careful for nothing; but in every thing by prayer and supplication with thanksgiving let your requests be made known unto God. And the peace of God, which passeth all understanding, shall keep your hearts and minds through Christ Jesus" (Phil 4:6–7).

In each counseling session, it is the hope of the counselor that the counselee(s) will come face to face with Christ through relevant biblical truths that will convict, comfort, guide, teach, and ultimately bring about genuine, lasting heart change. This is not possible under our own power or without the Holy Spirit's intervention. Thus, prayer is an essential component of counseling if the counselor desires the Holy Spirit's power to be at work in the counseling session.

Prayer accomplishes several things for you as a counselor: (a) It expresses to the Lord your desire for His fellowship and love. It shows your obedience to Him, your need for Him, your trust in Him, and your commitment to Him. (b) It prepares the counselees by softening hearts and making them more receptive to truth. (c) It impacts others through good works done by the counselor and the counselee to display the Lord's love and care.

In Christ's model prayer, following His adoration of the holiness and sovereignty of God the Father and words of submission to the Father's will, He petitions, "Give us this day our daily bread" (Matt 6:11). This request is in reference to our human needs and sets the example of praying for self. As God's servant, a counselor is in desperate need of God's provision: "Not that we are sufficient of ourselves to think anything as of ourselves; but our sufficiency is of God; who also hath made us able ministers of the new testament; not of the letter, but of the spirit: for the letter killeth, but the spirit giveth life" (2 Cor 3:5—6). In light of our inadequacies, the Lord reminds us that prayer is the avenue for approaching "the throne of grace" for obtaining "help in time of need" (Heb 4:16). The counselor needs biblical wisdom and an accurate understanding of the Scriptures as well as insight into the counselee's life. James tells us to ask God for wisdom: "If any of you lack wisdom, let him ask of God, that giveth to all men liberally, and upbraideth not; and it shall be given him" (James 1:5).

The psalmist recognized his need of the Holy Spirit's help in understanding God's Word as he cried out to God, "Open thou mine eyes, that I may behold wondrous things out of thy law" (Ps 119:18). The counselor ought to do the same. Paul asked the Ephesians to pray for him that words would be given to him so that he would "speak boldly as [he] ought to speak" (Eph 6:20). The counselor needs this same kind of help. And Jesus explained that the Holy Spirit would "bring all things to remembrance," speaking of those things that He had taught (John 14:26). The counselor will face many instances when he needs the Holy Spirit to bring to his remembrance relevant Scriptural truths that he has learned and memorized in the past. The Lord can even use verses from a trial or victory many years earlier.

The counselor invests time and effort in talking and studying with counselees, but his work is made effective only through the empowering of the Holy Spirit. It is the Holy Spirit who enables ministers of His Word to proclaim the Word (Acts 4:8, 31, 6:10; 1 Thess 1:5; 1 Pet 1:12), to overcome spiritual opposition, and to work in people's lives (Matt 12:28, Eph 6:17). In fact, it is the Holy Spirit who empowers the counselor's prayer and makes it effective (Rom. 8:26, Eph. 2:18). In addition, the gifts with which the counselor has been equipped for the ministry are given by the Holy Spirit (1 Cor. 12:11). Finally, the Holy Spirit speaks through the counselor's teaching of the Scriptures to the counselee's heart (Heb. 3:7, 10:15). Clearly, we can see why the counselor ought to begin by praying for his own ministry to the counselee.

As the counseling proceeds and God transforms the heart of the counselee, the counselor must be on guard against the temptation to take credit for the change being accomplished. The counselor must ask God for help to grow in humility and to remember to give God the glory.

Besides praying for himself in preparation for his ministry, the counselor ought to be praying for the counselee as well. People come to counseling because they are troubled. Often, they come to counseling because they see deficiencies in themselves in areas such as communication, relationships, and lack of self-control. The Bible commands, "Confess your faults one to another, and pray one for another, that ye may be healed. The effectual fervent prayer of a righteous man availeth much" (James 5:16).

Counselees need prayer. They have some hard work ahead of them. They will need a humble, teachable heart to confront their own sin. They need a heart prepared by the Holy Spirit to understand and receive the biblical truths taught. Like you, they need the power of the Holy Spirit to persevere in overcoming sinful patterns, despite fear, failure, frustration, weariness, and opposition. They need the wisdom to look to the Lord rather than to people or to changes in circumstances for their hope. As they learn more and more of God's principles for living, they, like the counselor, will need the Holy Spirit to bring to their remembrance the teaching of the Word in day-to-day living. This is the essence of God's work.

In his book *Competent to Counsel*, Jay Adams declares:

Chapter 2

> Counseling is the work of the Holy Spirit. Effective counseling cannot be done apart from him. He is called the paraclete [the theological term for the Holy Spirit as our advocate] who in Christ's place came to be another counselor of the same sort that Christ had been to his disciples. . . . Counseling, to be Christian, must be carried on in harmony with the regenerating and sanctifying work of the Spirit.[8]

Obviously, the Holy Spirit is essential if the counseling is going to bring about genuine lasting change in the counselee, and prayer is the counselor's and the counselee's avenue for petitioning God for His transforming power. Therefore, the prayers that accompany counseling should include the following petitions:

- For wisdom for both the counselor and counselee (James 1:5)
- For the illumination of God's Word by the Holy Spirit opening their eyes as they study the Bible (Ps 119:18)
- For the equipping of the counselor by the Holy Spirit (1 Cor 12:11)
- For the Holy Spirit's empowerment of the counselor to effectively proclaim the truths of Scripture to the counselee (Acts 4:8, 31; 6:10; 1 Thess 1:5; 1 Pet 1:12) and to overcome any spiritual opposition (Matt 12:28, Eph 6:17)
- For the preparation of the counselee's heart to receive the Holy Spirit's prompting through the teaching of the Word (Eph 5:19–20; Heb 3:7; 10:15)
- For the humility of both the counselor and the counselee so that they give God the glory for the work being accomplished (Acts 12:21–23, Luke 18:9–14, Prov 3:34, Dan 4:30–37).

The following are six scriptural principles that highlight the importance of prayer in the counseling process:

1. "Ask, and it shall be given you; seek, and ye shall find; knock, and it shall be opened unto you: For every one that asketh receiveth, and he that seeketh findeth, and to him that knocketh it shall be opened" (Matt 7:7–8). In these verses, Jesus encourages His followers to persist I petitioning the Lord in prayer. The assurance is that those who earnestly pursue God through prayer will receive answers and find what they are looking for.

2. "Be careful for nothing; but in everything by prayer and supplication with thanksgiving let your requests be made known unto God. And the peace of God, which passeth all understanding, shall keep your hearts and minds through Christ Jesus" (Phil 4:6–7). This passage emphasizes the importance of bringing all concerns and needs before God in prayer. When we do so, God's peace, which surpasses human understanding, guards our hearts and minds.

3. "Pray without ceasing" (1 Thess 5:17). This verse encourages believers to maintain a constant attitude of prayer, staying connected with God throughout their daily lives. Prayer is not just a religious ritual but a continuous conversation with the Lord.

4. Pray and "Ye shall receive power, after that the Holy Ghost is come upon you: and ye shall be witnesses unto me both in Jerusalem, and in all Judaea, and in Samaria, and unto the uttermost part of the earth" (Acts 1:8). Before ascending to heaven, Jesus promised the disciples that they would receive power from the Holy Spirit. This power enabled them to be effective witnesses for Christ, spreading the gospel to various regions.

5. "Likewise the Spirit also helpeth our infirmities: for we know not what we should pray for as we ought: but the Spirit itself maketh intercession for us with groanings which cannot be uttered" (Rom 8:26). The Holy Spirit assists believers in their weaknesses, including the times when they don't know how to pray or express their

needs adequately. The Spirit intercedes on behalf of believers, communicating their deepest concerns to God.

6. Pray for the right spirit, that "The fruit of the Spirit is love, joy, peace, longsuffering, gentleness, goodness, faith, meekness, temperance: against such, there is no law" (Gal 5:22–23). The Holy Spirit produces spiritual fruit in the lives of believers, transforming their character to reflect Christlikeness.

In summary, prayer is a powerful means through which believers can communicate with God, seek His will, and find comfort and peace in times of need. The Holy Spirit plays a pivotal role in empowering believers, guiding them in prayer, and transforming their lives to bear spiritual fruit that honors God. In biblical counseling, prayer is vital because it acknowledges the role of the Holy Spirit in the process. The counselor should seek God's guidance, wisdom, and discernment through prayer to understand the counselee's needs and to be led by the Holy Spirit throughout the counseling journey.

Examine yourself

In addition to seeking God in prayer for help in ministering to the counselee, the counselor should also seek God for help in the process of self-examination to determine where repentance and change are required in his own heart, ministry, and life. In the Sermon on the Mount, Jesus taught us that if we are going to attempt to help a brother or sister overcome sin, we must first get control of the sin in our own lives:

> Why beholdest thou the mote that is in thy brother's eye, but considerest not the beam that is in thine own eye? Or how wilt thou say to thy brother, Let me pull out the mote out of thine eye; and, behold, a beam is in thine own eye? Thou hypocrite, first cast out the beam out of thine own eye; and then shalt thou see clearly to cast out the mote out of thy brother's eye. (Matt 7:3–5)

Please understand that the need for self-examination does not mean that a counselor must be perfect and sinless. That is impossible in this earthly life. What the Lord is saying is that the counselor ought to be carefully evaluating his own heart and life, confessing sin to God and others whom he has offended as well as working daily to overcome known sin and sinful patterns. Additionally, a counselor's family and ministry should be a godly example of grace.

The step of examining yourself is essential to biblical counseling and involves you as the counselor introspectively evaluating your own life, motives, and spiritual condition before engaging with the counselee. The Bible provides insights on why self-examination is vital and how it plays a crucial role in effective biblical counseling.

Self-examination leads to recognition of our own limitations and our need for God's grace. Confessing that he was often blind to his own sin, David prayed: "Search me, O God, and know my heart: try me, and know my thoughts: and see if there be any wicked way in me, and lead me in the way everlasting" (Ps 139:23–24). David's prayer demonstrates the importance of asking God to examine his heart and thoughts. Engaging in self-examination helps counselors recognize their own shortcomings and sinful tendencies, allowing God to lead them on the path of righteousness. The prophet Jeremiah declared, "The heart is deceitful above all things, and desperately wicked: who can know it? I the LORD search the heart, I try the reins, even to give every man according to his ways, and according to the fruit of his doings" (Jer 17:9–10). This verse highlights the fallen nature of the human heart and the inherent need for self-awareness. By examining themselves, counselors acknowledge their potential biases, prejudices, and limitations, seeking God's help to overcome them.

Self-examination helps us cultivate humility and compassion. "Let nothing be done through strife or vainglory, but in lowliness of mind let each esteem other better than themselves. Look not every man on his own things, but every man also on the things of others" (Phil 2:3–4).

Biblical counselors must approach their role with humility, considering the needs and struggles of the counselee as more important than their own. Self-examination fosters sympathy, allowing counselors to genuinely identify with the counselees' experiences. "Brethren, if a man be overtaken in a fault, ye which are spiritual, restore such an one in the spirit of meekness; considering thyself, lest thou also be tempted. Bear ye one another's burdens, and so fulfil the law of Christ" (Gal 6:1–2). Self-examination reminds counselors of their own vulnerability to sin, prompting them to approach the counselee with gentleness and a desire to restore the individual. Understanding their own weaknesses helps counselors avoid being judgmental or critical.

Self-examination should reinforce a God-centered focus. "If ye then be risen with Christ, seek those things which are above, where Christ sitteth on the right hand of God. Set your affection on things above, not on things on the earth" (Col 3:1–2). Self-examination should not lead to self-reliance or pride but rather to a greater dependence on Christ. Counselors must continually seek God's guidance and align their focus on Him as they counsel. "For we preach not ourselves, but Christ Jesus the Lord; and ourselves your servants for Jesus' sake" (2 Cor 4:5). Biblical counselors should not promote themselves or their wisdom but instead focus on leading the counselee to Christ and His Word. Self-examination helps counselors check their motives, ensuring they are serving the counselee for Jesus' sake.

In summary, self-examination in biblical counseling involves acknowledging personal limitations, humbly sympathizing with the counselee, and staying God-centered in approach. It allows counselors to remove potential obstacles that might hinder their effectiveness and align their hearts with God's will to provide compassionate and Christ-centered guidance.

Two specific self-examination questions are particularly crucial.

Are you committed to the total sufficiency of Scripture? God inspired the Bible to provide authoritative guidance to his people as they honor

Him during our difficulties in this sinful, broken world. People seek counseling when life does not seem to be working properly and they need help understanding and addressing what has gone wrong. We believe it is the divine intention of Scripture to describe (a) the perfect standard to which people must conform as they live their lives, (b) the spiritual problems they face in life that challenge that standard, and (c) the process of transformation that God has designed to help them change. Biblical counselors are committed to using the Scriptures in counseling out of the conviction that the topics addressed in the Bible are the exact issues addressed in counseling conversations.

A commitment to the total sufficiency of Scripture means firmly believing that the Bible, as the Word of God, is completely adequate and comprehensive to address all matters of faith, life, and practice. It is the understanding that God's Word contains everything necessary for salvation, guidance, and spiritual growth. The Bible itself supports this perspective: "All scripture is given by inspiration of God, and is profitable for doctrine, for reproof, for correction, for instruction in righteousness: That the man of God may be perfect, thoroughly furnished unto all good works" (2 Tim 3:16–17). This well-known passage emphasizes that all Scripture is divinely inspired and beneficial for various aspects of the believer's life, including doctrine, correction, and instruction in righteousness. Through the Scriptures, the man or woman of God is equipped for every good work, indicating its comprehensive sufficiency.

Deuteronomy 8:3 says, "He humbled thee, and suffered thee to hunger, and fed thee with manna, which thou knewest not, neither did thy fathers know; that he might make thee know that man doth not live by bread only, but by every word that proceedeth out of the mouth of the LORD doth man live." With these words, Moses reminded the Israelites that life is sustained not only by physical food but also by every word that comes from the mouth of the Lord. This highlights the spiritual nourishment and sufficiency found in God's Word.

Many psalms also extol the perfection and completeness of God's law. "The law of the LORD is perfect, converting the soul: the testimony of the LORD is sure, making wise the simple. The statutes of the LORD are right, rejoicing the heart: the commandment of the LORD is pure, enlightening the eyes" (Ps 19:7–8). The law (God's Word) converts the soul, imparts wisdom, brings joy to the heart, and provides spiritual enlightenment. It is sufficient to bring about spiritual transformation and growth in the believer.

Proverbs 30:5 has a similar theme: "Every word of God is pure: he is a shield unto them that put their trust in him." The purity of Scripture is emphasized because every word from God is untainted and reliable. Those who trust in the Lord and His Word find Him to be their protector and shield. God's Word is powerful and effective. It always accomplishes His purposes and is fully sufficient to achieve the divine plan. "So shall my word be that goeth forth out of my mouth: it shall not return unto me void, but it shall accomplish that which I please, and it shall prosper in the thing whereto I sent it" (Isa 55:11).

In summary, a commitment to the total sufficiency of Scripture is firmly rooted in the belief that God's Word, as revealed in the Bible, is entirely adequate for guiding, instructing, and transforming the believer's life. It contains all that is needed for salvation, spiritual growth, and righteous living. By relying on God's Word and recognizing its completeness, believers find everything necessary to navigate life in obedience to God's will. Biblical counseling must be biblical!

What are your motives for counseling? Ensuring that your goal as a biblical counselor is solely to bring glory to the Lord by helping the counselee(s) is a fundamental principle that aligns with the teachings of the Bible. This motivation will shape your approach, attitude, and focus during the counseling process, prioritizing God's honor and the counselee's well-being above all else.

The church at Corinth was only a few years old when the apostle Paul wrote the letter we call 1 Corinthians. For perspective, consider that the problems we have in churches today are in many cases with people who have been saved for decades; this indicates how bad the young church at Corinth really was. That church was a mess when the Lord inspired Paul to deal with it.

Before Paul comments on what they are doing, he reminds them who they are. Instead of immediately addressing the condition of their lives, he causes them to stop and remember their position in Christ. The Corinthian believers had strayed from morality and God's desire for their lives. Having placed their faith in Him, they would always be His children, but currently they were bringing no glory to God.

In addition to this, Paul thanks God for these people. Many of them are ones he led to Christ and pastored when planting the church. Paul points out their God-given strengths and assures them of God's ability and faithfulness. He promises that they will be blameless when Jesus comes back (1 Cor 1:8). How can Paul say this when it's clear that their actions are reprehensible? Though their lives are characterized by blameworthy behavior, he promises that they will stand guiltless before God! The reason he can do that is because God is faithful. Paul isn't banking on their faithfulness or repentance but on God's character. Understanding that God's character is the key to our success changes things. The onus is not on us to save the world; it is on us to follow the only One who can do that and following Him well so that the honor and the glory for all our ministry successes goes to Him.

Believers should be motivated to bring glory to God in everything we do or choose not to do. This includes our choices to eat or drink or to abstain. Paul adds this to a list of motivating factors for the use of our freedom in Christ when he reminds the church: "Whether therefore ye eat, or drink, or whatsoever ye do, do all to the glory of God" (1 Cor 10:31). In all cases, the question of whether a certain activity will bring you pleasure, material gain, or status should not be the sole deciding factor even for those who are free in Christ. Just as anything done "not of faith is sin" (Rom 14:23), Christians should not participate in anything they don't think brings glory to God. Paul is emphasizing the all-encompassing nature of bringing glory to God in every aspect of life, including counseling. By directing counselees' intentions and actions toward God's glory, the counselor prioritizes God's will above personal agendas, achievements, or recognition.

Many other passages support this understanding the role of motivation in biblical counseling. "Let your light so shine before men, that they may see your good works, and glorify your Father which is in heaven" (Matt 5:16). Biblical counselors should strive to let their lights shine before others, including their counselee(s), through the actions they take and the guidance they offer. By seeking to bring glory to God in their counseling efforts, counselors reflect God's love and truth, leading counselee(s) to glorify the heavenly Father.

Biblical counselors should conduct themselves in word and deed in a manner that reflects the Lord Jesus. "Whatsoever ye do in word or deed, do all in the name of the Lord Jesus, giving thanks to God and the Father by him" (Col 3:17). By helping the counselee(s) cultivate a heart of gratitude to God, the counselor acknowledges God's sovereignty and authority over the counseling process.

"If any man speak, let him speak as the oracles of God; if any man minister, let him do it as of the ability which God giveth: that God in all things may be glorified through Jesus Christ, to whom be praise and dominion for ever and ever" (1 Pet 4:11). The biblical counselor should counsel and minister in accordance with God's Word and the ability provided by God. By doing so, the focus remains on God's glory, and God is honored through Jesus Christ.

The motivation to please God rather than seeking approval from men is central to biblical counseling. "For do I now persuade men, or God? Or do I seek to please men? For if I yet pleased men, I should not be the servant of Christ" (Gal 1:10). By seeking to serve Christ faithfully in counseling, the counselor prioritizes God's approval above human recognition.

The proverb says, "Commit thy works unto the LORD, and thy thoughts shall be established." When biblical counselors commit their work of counseling to the Lord, they invite His guidance and direction. This ensures that their thoughts and motivations align with God's will, ultimately seeking to bring Him glory through the counseling process.

In summary, ensuring that the motivation of a biblical counselor is solely to bring glory to the Lord by helping counselees reflects the counselor's commitment to prioritize God's honor and the counselee's well-being above personal ambitions. By seeking to align their actions, words, and thoughts with God's will, counselors magnify God's name through their counseling efforts and exemplify Christlike love and compassion toward those they counsel.

Practical Preparation (Logistical)

Logistics includes dealing with the details of securing an appropriate space where the counseling can take place, obtaining the necessary information from counselees about themselves and their situations, and complying with the relevant reporting requirements.

Select an appropriate space

Preparing logistically and having a suitable counseling space can significantly contribute to the effectiveness and success of the biblical counseling process. While the Bible does not specifically mention the practical aspects of counseling, it provides principles and teachings that align with the importance of organization, orderliness, and creating an environment conducive to counseling. Be sure you have adequate insurance for all biblical counseling activities. Let's explore how preparing logistics and having a great space can help biblical counseling.

- **A physical location**

The best place to counsel someone is in a professional office space. This provides a clean, quiet, safe, and comfortable environment. Additionally, it allows for the counselor to have the necessary computer equipment, books, supplies, and so on. It's good to have a supply of water and coffee available. Personally, I believe the best location for counseling is always within the jurisdiction of the church because counselees should be required to attend at least one service per week, non-negotiable. At times you may need to go into a home or meet in some other safe, quiet, private location, I do not recommend that a biblical counselor ever be alone in a building with a counselee. Under no circumstances should a biblical counselor be behind closed doors alone with someone of the opposite gender or with a child. Always arrange for a partner to be present. I believe that the spouse of the counselor is normally the best counseling partner when dealing with the opposite gender counselee or a child. Here are a few details and biblical principles to consider when selecting and preparing a physical location.

Orderliness and preparation. "Let all things be done decently and in order" (1 Cor 14:40). This verse emphasizes the importance of conducting things properly and in an orderly manner. Being organized and well-prepared in areas such as the scheduling of appointments, working from a structured counseling plan, and providing relevant resources all help maintain an orderly and well-managed counseling process.

An atmosphere of comfort and trust. A great counseling space should be inviting and comfortable, fostering an atmosphere of trust and openness. Pleasant surroundings and a relaxed setting can help the counselee feel at ease, making them more receptive to guidance and counsel. "Pleasant words are as an honeycomb, sweet to the soul, and health to the bones" (Prov 16:24). In addition, a well-prepared counseling space allows for multiple counselors or advisors to participate in the process if necessary. This can provide diverse perspectives and ensure the counselee receives comprehensive and balanced guidance. As Proverbs 11:14 says, "In the multitude of counsellors there is safety."

Practicality and accessibility. "The thoughts of the diligent tend only to plenteousness; but of every one that is hasty only to want" (Prov 21:5). Diligence in preparing logistics and having a suitable space ensures that the counseling sessions are well managed and fruitful. It allows the counselor to have the necessary resources at hand, making the process more effective.

Confidentiality and privacy. A great counseling space also provides confidentiality and privacy for the counselee. This helps build trust, as counselees feel safe to share their struggles and concerns without fear of their personal information being divulged. "He that goeth about as a talebearer revealeth secrets: therefore meddle not with him that flattereth with his lips" (Prov 20:19).

To sum up, the counselor should ensure the practical aspects of counseling are prepared, such as setting up a suitable counseling space, scheduling sessions, and making necessary arrangements to facilitate an effective counseling environment. By preparing in advance and creating a great counseling space, biblical counselors can set a positive tone for the counseling process, fostering an environment that encourages openness, trust, and a focus on God's Word. Such an atmosphere helps ensure that the counsel provided aligns with biblical principles and leads the counselee towards spiritual growth and healing.

- **An online connection**

Counseling someone over the phone or via the internet (using a program such as Zoom) can have numerous benefits, including accessibility (connecting online allows people to seek help from the comfort of their own homes or any location with internet access), convenience (scheduling and attending online counseling sessions is easier, especially for those with busy schedules or limited mobility), privacy (online sessions offer a level of privacy and confidentiality when they are conducted in a secure virtual environment), anonymity (clients may feel more comfortable discussing sensitive or personal issues online), flexibility (having more options in terms of session timing and duration can accommodate varying needs and preferences), efficiency (eliminating the need for travel to a physical location saves time and money and reduces potential stress), and opportunity (online counseling enables individuals to access counselors from different locations, expanding the range of available expertise).

Online counseling sessions should follow all the conditions already stipulated. In addition, the counselor should (1) use a secure, encrypted communication platform to conduct online sessions, protecting client information from unauthorized access, (2) establish boundaries by clearly communicating the necessity of confidentiality and informing clients about the limitations of online security, and (3) obtain explicit informed consent from clients, explaining the risks and benefits of online counseling, including potential privacy concerns.

Compile data on the counselee

Compiling data on a counselee is a critical step in biblical counseling, as it provides valuable insights into their background, struggles, and needs. The Bible underscores the significance of understanding others' situations and seeking God's guidance in offering counsel. Therefore, prior to counseling, a counselor should gather some pertinent facts about the potential counselee.

Why to collect data. Purposes for collecting data include (a) discerning whether you should counsel this person, (b) ascertaining the counselee's spiritual condition, and (c) identifying his or her problems biblically. Having this information will enable you present biblical solutions and to give appropriate homework assignments. Use a pre-counseling questionnaire to review prior to counseling. I have provided an example in Appendix E.

a. Always ask for the Lord's guidance regarding whether you should counsel a particular person or people. Gathering relevant information about counselees will help you understand their situation better. However, the decision to counsel someone should also be guided by seeking God's direction since not every case will be appropriate for biblical counseling. Spiritual discernment is essential. "If any of you lack wisdom, let him ask of God, that giveth to all men liberally, and upbraideth not; and it shall be given him" (James 1:5). Compiling data is an opportunity for the counselor to pray for wisdom and discernment from God. By seeking His guidance, the counselor relies on God's knowledge to offer the most appropriate counsel and to determine who is the right person to provide it.

Proverbs 3:5-6 admonishes the counselor, "Trust in the LORD with all thine heart; and lean not unto thine own understanding. In all thy ways acknowledge him, and he shall direct thy paths." Seeking God's guidance in counseling decisions is crucial. Compiling data is not merely about gathering information but acknowledging the need for divine direction. God's wisdom surpasses human understanding, and seeking His guidance ensures that the counselor follows His plan in the counseling process.

b. Determine if the counselee is a Christian. Understanding a counselee's spiritual status is essential in biblical counseling because it directly influences the approach, guidance, and counsel that will be provided by the counselor. The Bible emphasizes the significance of discerning people's spiritual condition and how it shapes their needs, struggles, and ultimate solutions. "Jesus answered and said unto [Nicodemus], Verily, verily, I say unto thee, Except a man be born again, he cannot see the kingdom of God" (John 3:3). This verse highlights the necessity of being born again to enter the kingdom of God. Biblical counseling seeks to address both the spiritual and practical needs of counselees, and understanding their spiritual status is fundamental to tailor the counsel accordingly.

Knowing whether counselees are believers in Christ allows the counselor to understand their spiritual needs better. "The LORD is nigh unto them that are of a broken heart; and saveth such as be of a contrite spirit" (Ps 34:18). Those who are spiritually broken or contrite may require specific biblical principles, such as repentance, forgiveness, and restoration through faith in Jesus Christ. Someone who is not saved will perceive little to no value in biblical counseling. Once a person is saved, he or she will gain the help of the Holy Spirit of the Lord in healing: "The natural man receiveth not the things of the Spirit of God: for they are foolishness unto him: neither can he know them, because they are spiritually discerned" (1 Cor 2:14). An understanding of counselees' spiritual status helps the counselor recognize if they are likely to be receptive to biblical truths. Nonbelievers (the "natural man") may struggle to grasp spiritual concepts without the work of the Holy Spirit in their hearts.

Since Biblical counseling relies on God's Word as the source of guidance and instruction, understanding counselees' spiritual status helps the counselor apply appropriate biblical teachings, relevant to their relationship with God and level of spiritual understanding. "All scripture is given by inspiration of God, and is profitable for doctrine, for reproof, for correction, for instruction in righteousness: That the man of God may be perfect, thoroughly furnished unto all good works" (2 Tim 3:16–17).

As Paul says, "Let the word of Christ dwell in you richly in all wisdom; teaching and admonishing one another in psalms and hymns and spiritual songs, singing with grace in your hearts to the Lord" (Col 3:16). Knowing counselees' spiritual status enables the counselor to urge them to immerse themselves in God's Word. For believers, the Word of Christ dwells richly and plays a significant role in their lives, shaping their thoughts and actions.

Finally, understanding counselees' spiritual status also allows the counselor to provide appropriate discipleship. With nonbelievers, the focus will be on explaining the gospel and guiding them toward accepting Christ. With believers, the emphasis is on helping them grow in their faith and obedience to God's commands: "Go ye therefore, and teach all nations, baptizing them in the name of the Father, and of the Son, and of the Holy Ghost: Teaching them to observe all things whatsoever I have commanded you: and, lo, I am with you always, even unto the end of the world" (Matt 28:19–20). Knowing a counselee's spiritual status enables the counselor to offer appropriate restoration and encouragement. The approach may differ for a believer struggling with sin compared to someone who is yet to accept Christ. "Brethren, if a man be overtaken in a fault, ye which are spiritual, restore such an one in the spirit of meekness; considering thyself, lest thou also be tempted" (Gal 6:1). (Note: Personally, I will not counsel an individual who does not attend a Bible believing church at least once per week.)

c. Seek to understand each counselee's situation from a biblical perspective. As Solomon advised, "He that answereth a matter before he heareth it, it is folly and shame unto him" (Prov 18:13). Before providing counsel, it is essential to hear and understand the counselee's situation as fully as possible. Compiling data allows the counselor to develop a comprehensive picture of the counselee's struggles, ensuring that the counsel provided is well-informed and relevant. Compiling data also involves drawing out the deeper issues and concerns within the counselees' hearts. "Counsel in the heart of man is like deep water; but a man of understanding will draw it out" (Prov 20:5). By understanding the root causes of their challenges, the counselor can address them effectively with biblical wisdom.

In summary, compiling data on a counselee is indispensable in biblical counseling. It enables the counselor to gain a comprehensive understanding of the counselees' situation, seek God's guidance in the counseling process, and tailor the counsel to address both their practical and spiritual needs. By diligently gathering relevant information and seeking God's wisdom, the counselor can provide effective, God-honoring counsel that leads the counselee towards healing and spiritual growth.

What data to collect. At a minimum, you should have the following types of information on file:

Full name (and maiden name, if applicable)
Emergency contact information
Address, phone number, and email address.
Medical information (e.g., doctor's name and phone number)
Church information (e.g., name and location, pastor's name and phone number)

In summary, understanding the counselees' spiritual status and general situation in life is crucial in biblical counseling because it helps the counselor address their spiritual needs, tailor biblical guidance, provide relevant discipleship, and offer appropriate restoration and encouragement. By discerning where the counselee stands in relationship with God, the counselor can effectively apply God's Word to lead the person toward healing, growth, and a deeper understanding of God's truth and grace.

Comply with mandatory reporting requirements

What does the Bible say? "Let every soul be subject unto the higher powers. For there is no power but of God: the powers that be are ordained of God" (Rom 13:1). The Lord clearly tells us we have a responsibility to government to follow its rules. Simply stated, we are to obey the laws of those appointed over us, whether we like them or not. God appoints a nation's leaders, but not always to bless the people. Sometimes, it is to judge the people or to prepare the nation for judgment.

In light of that, this section gives a simple overview of the mandatory reporting requirements as they apply to biblical counselors. The review is a summary of requirements taken from meetings, state codes, and classes. Most state laws are consistent with one another; however, you have the obligation to familiarize yourself with laws affecting your local ministry and to be sure you understand them. In most cases, you can find a comprehensive list online or through local counseling organizations or legal groups that serve Christian counselors. One such group is the Christian Law Association (www.christianlaw.org/cla/), whose mission is to help local churches and Christian organizations stay blameless by meeting the requirements of the law.

(In no way should the following brief overview be considered legal advice. It is intended only for informational purposes and to help you understand that before entering a counseling/small group environment, you have municipal, county, state, and national requirements as a reporter. Please review your local, state, and national requirements prior to counseling. Also, I would like to remind you that you have an ultimate responsibility to your Lord. In every circumstance you are to remain blameless and in compliance with the law. As a Christian, you must strive in all you do to bring Him honor and glory. Hiding or concealing information is evil.)

Mandatory reporting laws began in California in the 1960s. Initially the laws applied just to children and have now expanded to include all vulnerable people. All fifty states, the District of Columbia, and US territories have mandatory reporter laws in some form. In some states the requirements fall under laws about not reporting a crime. When a crime is not reported, the more severe the crime, the more severe the punishment is for not reporting it.

Who is a mandatory reporter? A mandatory reporter is anyone in regular contact with vulnerable people such as children, the infirm, ill, abused, suicidal persons, mentally ill, disabled persons, veterans, people with PTSD, students, or those placed in a position where they can be taken advantage of. Mandatory reporters are legally required to report (or cause a report to be made) when abuse is observed or suspected. This abuse may include but is not limited to financial, physical, sexual, neglect, or mental abuse and also applies to people suspected of potentially hurting themselves. Mandatory reporters play a key role in the government's effort to protect people in need by identifying possible maltreatment and reporting it to the agencies responsible for investigation and intervention.

What are the requirements? As a mandatory reporter, if during counseling or small-group interaction you uncover the possibility of abuse, you must take the following actions:

- Contact the local authorities immediately. I recommend you call 911. Only the police can determine statutes of limitation or false reports.

- Do everything in your power to ensure the safety of the abused person until the proper authorities take over the situation.

- Safeguard all information with complete privacy. Do not share details with anyone but the authorities. If necessary, and only under the direction of the authorities, you may have to check with others in your church or group for suspected abuse or for details to help an investigation.

What happens if you fail to report? A mandated reporter, including a clergy member, who knowingly fails to report a crime or neglect can be found guilty of a misdemeanor (or felony in some states) and possibly serve jail time. In most cases, clergy or counselors found guilty of covering a crime will never be able to be insured again in a like position. If appropriate, they may be placed on a child abusers watch list. More importantly they are violating the Lord's requirement in Romans 13.

What if the authorities fail to act? If after reporting a crime, you suspect local authorities are not complying with the law, you are required to report the crime to a higher authority.

What about confidentiality and immunity from liability? US law requires law enforcement to keep the identity of the reporter confidential. The law provides only limited instances when the identity of the reporter may be revealed. For example, it may be revealed to other organizations to aid in the prosecution of the accused. In almost all cases, the law creates a rebuttable presumption that mandatory reporters have acted in good faith by reporting abuse or neglect. Persons required or permitted to report suspected abuse or neglect, or who participate in an investigation or court proceeding because of a report, are immune from civil and criminal liability, provided that such persons acted in good faith. Immunity covers full disclosure of all facts that led the person to believe or suspect that a child or other person has been or may be abused or neglected.

A mandated reporter statement is essential for establishing the counselor's legal and ethical responsibilities. It ensures that the counselee understands that if any situation arises during counseling that requires reporting to authorities, the counselor will fulfill his or her obligation to protect the abused person.

A checklist outlining these steps can be helpful to ensure that the biblical counselor systematically addresses each area and provides holistic and effective guidance to the counselee(s) based on the principles found in the Bible. (Appendix D provides a worksheet to be used as a convenient tool for counselors to stay organized and thorough in the session.)

---

[8] Jay E. Adams, Competent to Counsel, Introduction to Nouthetic Counseling, Zondervan, Grand Rapids, MI (1970): 20

Do you understand everything you have read in this chapter?
If not, please read it again before moving on to Chapter 3.

CHAPTER 3

Understanding Human Nature and Sin

In practical terms, biblical counseling focuses on getting to the heart of the matter rather than merely dealing with surface-level behaviors. It aims to understand and address the underlying issues that drive thoughts, emotions, and actions, leading to lasting transformation and growth.

Understanding Human Nature and Sin

In biblical counseling, it is necessary to have a scriptural perspective on human nature, and the impact of sin and humanity's need for redemption. Below are twenty salient points in this biblical worldview presented as succinct statements of what the counselor should think or do as a result of seeing everything through this lens.

- **The Image of God:** Recognize that every individual is created in the image of God and thus possesses inherent dignity, value, and worth.

- **The Fall of Humanity:** Affirm the Genesis account of the fall and accept that it resulted in the entrance of sin into the world and the brokenness of human nature.

- **Humanity's Inherent Sinfulness:** Acknowledge the biblical teaching that sin has morally corrupted every aspect of human nature, including our thoughts, emotions, desires, and actions.

- **Guilt and Consequences of Sin:** Explore the reality of guilt and the consequences of sin in the lives of individuals, leading to pain, brokenness, and separation from God.

- **The Struggle with Sin:** Recognize the ongoing battle with sin in the lives of believers and nonbelievers alike and the need for both to continually rely on God's grace.

- **Repentance and Forgiveness:** Emphasize the importance of genuine repentance and the assurance of forgiveness through Christ's sacrifice.

- **The Role of the Law:** Understand the purpose of God's law in revealing sin and pointing people to the Savior they need.

- **Redemption through Christ:** Highlight the central message of the gospel, which offers redemption, forgiveness, and reconciliation through faith in Jesus Christ.

- **Justification and Sanctification:** Distinguish between justification (being declared righteous through faith in Christ) and sanctification (undergoing the process of becoming more Christlike).

- **The Role of the Holy Spirit:** Realize that it is the work of the Holy Spirit to convict of sin, to empower believers to overcome sin, and to produce godly character.

- **Receiving God's Grace and Mercy:** Emphasize God's abundant grace and mercy, which offer hope and transformation to those who turn to Him in repentance.

- **Finding identity in Christ:** Help individuals understand their new identity as children of God through faith in Christ and how it impacts their self-worth and purpose.

- **Overcoming Shame and Regret:** Assist people to apply the healing power of God's love and forgiveness to their feelings of shame and regret.

- **Renewing the Mind:** Encourage the renewal of the mind through the study and application of God's Word, leading to transformed thinking and behavior.

- **Coping with Temptation:** Equip individuals with biblical strategies to resist temptation and rely on God's strength to overcome sin.

- **Extending Grace to Others:** Encourage individuals to extend grace and forgiveness to others, reflecting the love and mercy they have received from God.

- **Healing from Past Wounds:** Guide individuals through the process of healing from the wounds of sin and brokenness, finding restoration in Christ.

- **Living a Spirit-Filled Life:** Teach believers to walk in the Spirit, relying on His guidance and empowerment to lead them away from sin and toward godliness.

- **Cultivating Repentant Hearts:** Model an attitude of humility and repentance before God, recognizing our ongoing need for His forgiveness and grace.

- **Embracing the Journey of Redemption:** Stress that the journey of understanding human nature, sin, and redemption is a lifelong process of growing in God's grace and becoming more like Christ.

Now we'll consider each category in detail.

The Image of God

The phrase "image of God" refers to the inherent dignity, value, and unique qualities that every individual possesses as a result of being created in the likeness of God. This biblical concept is foundational in understanding human nature and forms the basis for compassionate and respectful counseling. The foundation for this way of thinking comes from both the Old Testament and the New.

Genesis 1:27 says, "God created man in his own image, in the image of God created he him; male and female created he them." Affirming that human beings are created in the image of God establishes their special and sacred status among the rest of God's creation.

The psalmist exults, "I will praise thee; for I am fearfully and wonderfully made: marvelous are thy works, and that my soul knoweth right well," expressing the awe and wonder of having been specially and created by the God who spoke the universe into existence. This highlights the unique value and purpose of each human being.

The New Testament reiterates the same theme in reference to those who are followers of Christ: "For we are his workmanship, created in Christ Jesus unto good works, which God hath before ordained that we should walk in them" (Eph 2:10). Believers are considered to be the product of God's amazing craftsmanship, designed for the purpose of carrying out God's plans. Understanding this truth can bring hope and direction into the counseling process.

The concept of the image of God in man may be explained as the inherent worth and potential of every human being. It acknowledges that individuals possess unique abilities, reasoning, and emotions that set them apart from other creatures. But how can this concept be incorporated into our biblical counseling practices?

Realizing that the recognition of the image of God in every individual is vital for establishing a foundation of respect and compassion, counselors can integrate this understanding in the following five ways:

1. *Affirming inherent worth.* Emphasize to counselees that they are valuable and cherished creations of God, deserving of dignity and respect.

2. *Nurturing realistic self-identity.* Help counselees explore and understand their God-given identity, acknowledging their unique qualities and potential in Christ. This will build a healthy self-concept based on internal (spiritual) factors rather than external (circumstantial) ones.

3. *Encouraging personal growth.* Assist counselees in realizing their purpose and potential in carrying out God's good works, fostering a sense of fulfillment and direction.

4. *Respecting diversity.* Recognize and celebrate the diversity among God's creatures, acknowledging the unique expressions of the Image of God in different individuals, cultures, ethnicities, and languages.

5. *Instilling hope.* Remind counselees that their worth and value come from being created in God's image, offering hope and encouragement in times of struggle.

By integrating this understanding of the image of God into their counseling, biblical counselors can foster a positive self-concept in counselees, inspire personal growth, and affirm the intrinsic value of each person, generating an environment of love, acceptance, and grace.

The Fall of Humanity

The term fall refers to what happened (as recorded in the biblical book of Genesis) when Adam and Eve, the first human beings, disobeyed God's command and introduced sin into the world. This pivotal event led to the brokenness of human nature and the need for redemption and restoration through Jesus Christ.

Moses, the writer of Genesis, tells the story:

> When the woman saw that the tree was good for food, and that it was pleasant to the eyes, and a tree to be desired to make one wise, she took of the fruit thereof, and did eat, and gave also unto her husband with her; and he did eat. And the eyes of them both were opened, and they knew that they were naked; and they sewed fig leaves together, and made themselves aprons. (Gen 3:6–7)

This moment of disobedience when Adam and Eve ate the forbidden fruit led to their realization of sin, which is why they attempted to cover their shame.

Adam's sin had far-reaching consequences since sin entered the world through him, affecting all humanity and leading to spiritual and physical death: "As by one man sin entered into the world, and death by sin; and so death passed upon all men, for that all have sinned" (Rom 5:12). Not only that, but all humans since then have sinned and fallen short of God's perfect standard, which clarifies the universal need for redemption through Christ. "All have sinned, and come short of the glory of God" (Rom 3:23).

The fall of humanity is a historical event that marks the origin of human suffering, moral imperfection, and brokenness. But what does that have to do with counseling? Understanding the significance of the fall is essential to biblical counseling for several reasons. By identifying the origin of all human struggles, biblical counseling acknowledges the presence of sin and brokenness in human nature, which underlies many of the challenges and struggles people face. This, in turn, allows the counselor to help counselees understand the source of their own guilt and shame, which may stem from the awareness of their fallen nature and past mistakes. Having pinpointed the root problem, the counselor can present the hope of redemption and restoration through Jesus Christ, who offers forgiveness and new life to all who believe in Him. A counselee who responds with humility, recognizing his or her own need for God's grace will be more likely to extend grace to others who also struggle with sin. By assisting counselees to find healing and wholeness through their relationship with God and His transformative power, the counselor can remind them that even though the fallen state of the world leads to trials and suffering, God offers comfort and strength through His presence.

Thus, by integrating this understanding of the fall of humanity into their counseling, biblical counselors can address the root of human struggles, provide hope and healing through Christ, and guide individuals toward a deeper relationship with God for lasting transformation and restoration.

Humanity's Inherent Sinfulness

The Bible teaches that all humanity is inherently sinful and morally corrupt due to the fall of Adam and Eve in the Garden of Eden. This fallen nature separates people from God and means they have an inborn propensity to sin. Scripture is clear concerning the inherent sinful nature of men and women, even from birth, as a result of the fall. David laments, "Behold, I was shapen in iniquity, and in sin did my mother conceive me" (Ps 51:5). Paul quotes two other psalms to reinforce the same point: "As it is written, There is none righteous, no, not one: There is none that understandeth, there is none that seeketh after God. They are all gone out of the way, they are together become unprofitable; there is none that doeth good, no, not one" (Rom 3:10–12). These verses affirm that all people have fallen into sin and have become morally corrupt, apart from the intervention of God's grace. The prophet Jeremiah agrees and emphasizes the deceitful and wicked nature of the human heart, which can lead to moral corruption and sinful behaviors: "The heart is deceitful above all things, and desperately wicked: who can know it?" (Jer 17:9).

Some people view human nature as complex and influenced by various factors such as genetics, environment, and upbringing. While others may acknowledge the presence of moral shortcomings, the concept of inherent sinfulness may not align with their beliefs. But in biblical counseling, both counselor and counselee must understand that the concept of inherent sinfulness and moral corruption is crucial in biblical counseling. Recognizing that human struggles and shortcomings are rooted in the fallen nature can enable counselors to address the core issues behind surface behaviors so they can help individuals understand their need for redemption and reconciliation with God through Jesus Christ's sacrifice.

Inviting counselees to receive God's grace and forgiveness for their sins promotes healing and restoration. Counselors should steer clear of moral relativism by upholding biblical principles and standards even when they are contrary to prevailing secular beliefs. Encouraging individuals to take responsibility for their actions while relying on God's strength to resist temptation and overcome sin and providing accountability will promote personal growth as you assist counselees in pursuing godly character and virtue, guided by the transformative power of God's Word and the Holy Spirit.

By integrating the understanding of inherent sinfulness and moral corruption into biblical counseling, counselors can offer hope, healing, and a clear path to redemption through Christ. This approach fosters humility, accountability, and a deeper reliance on God's grace and transformational power to overcome sinful tendencies and live a life that honors Him.

Guilt and Consequences of Sin

The Bible teaches that sin brings guilt and has serious consequences in the lives of individuals. Guilt arises from the awareness of having violated God's moral standard, leading to a sense of separation from Him. The other consequences of sin include personal, relational, and spiritual repercussions.

Romans 3:23 ("For all have sinned, and come short of the glory of God") highlights the universal reality of sin in all human beings, resulting in a sense of missing the mark of God's perfect standard. Another spiritual consequence of sin is that this separation between individuals and God hinders their prayers: "Your iniquities have separated between you and your God, and your sins have hid his face from you, that he will not hear" (Isa 59:2). David echoes the same sentiment: "I acknowledged my sin unto thee, and mine iniquity have I not hid. I said, I will confess my transgressions unto the Lord, and thou forgavest the iniquity of my sin" (Ps 32:5). This psalm illustrates not only the experience of guilt when a sin has been committed but also the relief and forgiveness received through confession and repentance.

Guilt may be viewed in psychological terms as a sense of remorse or regret for wrongdoing. Consequences of sinful actions are often seen as merely natural outcomes of behavior without reference to a higher moral authority, but that connection is essential.

Understanding guilt and the other consequences of sin is crucial in biblical counseling. Recognizing that guilt is usually a symptom of underlying sin and moral convictions helps counselees grasp their need for reconciliation with God. Assisting counselees to acknowledge their guilt and confess their sins before God can lead to their experiencing His forgiveness and restoration.

By encouraging individuals to take responsibility for their own actions and decisions, recognizing the impact of sin on themselves and others, counselors provide hope and healing, pointing them to God's abundant grace and mercy with the assurance that forgiveness and redemption are available through Christ.

As counselees make positive changes in their lives in alignment with God's Word, they can avoid additional harmful consequences of sin and pursue righteousness. Assisting individuals to process and resolve feelings of guilt and shame leads to emotional healing and freedom in Christ.

By integrating the understanding of guilt and the consequences of sin into biblical counseling, counselors can lead individuals to experience God's forgiveness, embrace accountability, and find hope and healing in Christ. This approach fosters spiritual growth, personal responsibility, and a deeper relationship with God.

The Struggle with Sin

The Bible acknowledges that both believers and nonbelievers experience a struggle with sin. Although believers are justified through faith in Jesus Christ, they continue to wrestle with the influence of sin in their lives. This struggle is a result of the fallen nature and the ongoing battle between the flesh and the Spirit. The apostle Paul candidly expressed his inner struggle with sin, even as a believer, recognizing the tension between his desire to do good and his inability to always fulfill it: "For I know that in me (that is, in my flesh,) dwelleth no good thing: for to will is present with me; but how to perform that which is good I find not. For the good that I would I do not: but the evil which I would not, that I do" (Rom 7:18–19). He also highlighted the conflict between the sinful nature (flesh) and the influence of the Holy Spirit in the life of a believer, resulting in an ongoing struggle with sin: "For the flesh lusteth against the Spirit, and the Spirit against the flesh: and these are contrary the one to the other: so that ye cannot do the things that ye would" (Gal 5:17).

The apostle John warned, "If we say that we have no sin, we deceive ourselves, and the truth is not in us" (1 John 1:8). The Bible acknowledges that all human beings, including believers, have the potential to sin, indicating the continuous struggle with sin. In secular terms, this problem may be understood as the human struggle to overcome negative behaviors, destructive habits, or harmful thought patterns. It is typically attributed to psychological, social, or environmental factors rather than to spiritual realities.

A biblical understanding of the struggle with sin is critical to effective counseling. The counselor should normalize the struggle, helping individuals recognize that the conflict is a common experience for all, and it does not mean they are failures or inadequate.

A biblical counselor will also assure counselees of God's abundant grace and forgiveness, encouraging them to turn to God in repentance and seek His strength in their weakness, and guide believers to rely on the empowering presence of the Holy Spirit to overcome sinful tendencies and live in obedience to God.

In addition to assisting individuals to identifying triggers that lead to sin and to develop healthy coping mechanisms to resist temptation, the biblical counselor will encourage them to seek support from a faith community, mentors, or accountability partners to aid in their journey of overcoming sin. Counselees need to have humility and recognize that transformation is a process requiring God's grace and ongoing growth in sanctification.

By integrating the scriptural understanding of the struggle with sin in biblical counseling, counselors can help individuals find hope, strength, and victory in their walk with God. This approach promotes self-awareness, reliance on God's grace, and a deepening relationship with the Holy Spirit to navigate the challenges of temptation and pursue godliness.

Repentance and Forgiveness

Repentance and forgiveness are fundamental aspects of dealing with sin from a biblical standpoint. Repentance involves a change of heart and mind, turning away from sinful behavior and turning toward God. Forgiveness is the gracious act of God, through Jesus Christ, in which He pardons the sins of those who genuinely repent and seek His mercy. "Repent ye therefore, and be converted, that your sins may be blotted out when the times of refreshing shall come from the presence of the Lord" (Acts 3:19). This verse calls for repentance and conversion, emphasizing that when individuals turn to God in genuine repentance, their sins will be forgiven, and they will experience spiritual refreshment. John expresses it as a promise: "If we confess our sins, he is faithful and just to forgive us our sins, and to cleanse us from all unrighteousness" (1 John 1:9). Jesus commanded "that repentance and remission of sins should be preached in his name among all nations, beginning at Jerusalem" (Luke 24:47). This commission highlights the centrality of repentance and forgiveness in the gospel message.

In psychological terms, repentance and forgiveness may be understood as a process of acknowledging wrongdoing, taking responsibility, and seeking reconciliation or relief from guilt and emotional distress. But it is only in the Lord that true forgiveness takes place. Understanding repentance and forgiveness in biblical counseling is vital for the following six reasons: (1) It facilitates personal responsibility, encouraging individuals to take ownership of their actions and acknowledge their sins before God and others. (2) It promotes emotional healing, assisting individuals to deal with their guilt and shame to experience the liberating power of God's forgiveness. (3) It encourages humility when people recognize their need for His grace. (4) It reinforces the truth of God's unconditional love and willingness to forgive those who genuinely repent. (5) It provides a path to reconciliation. This biblical truth guides counselees in seeking reconciliation with God and others, fostering healthier relationships. (6) It emphasizes the power of Christ's sacrifice by pointing individuals to the redemptive work of Jesus Christ on the cross, through which forgiveness and reconciliation are made possible.

By integrating the understanding of repentance and forgiveness into biblical counseling, counselors can lead individuals to experience the transformative power of God's forgiveness and embrace the freedom found in genuine repentance. This approach fosters emotional healing, spiritual growth, and a deeper relationship with God, leading to a life marked by grace and compassion towards others.

The Role of the Law

The Old Testament law consists of the commandments and statutes given by God to guide His people in righteous living and to reveal their sinfulness. It served as a tutor, pointing people to their need for a Savior (Christ) as they recognized their inability to perfectly keep the rules. "The law was our schoolmaster to bring us unto Christ, that we might be justified by faith" (Gal 3:24). The law makes people aware of their need for God's grace and forgiveness through faith in Jesus Christ because "by the deeds of the law there shall no flesh be justified in his sight: for by the law is the knowledge of sin" (Rom 3:20). Paul explains, "I had not known sin, but by the law: for I had not known lust, except the law had said, Thou shalt not covet" (Rom 7:7). The law clarifies what is right and wrong in God's eyes, leading individuals to understand their sinful tendencies and the need for redemption.

The law may be seen as a system of rules and regulations created by societies or governments to maintain order and establish moral standards, but the Bible teaches that it was given by God for the good of man (Deut 10:13).

It is essential that the biblical counselor understand the proper, multifaceted role of the law. It convicts of sin because it serves as a mirror that reflects human imperfection, highlighting the need for repentance and redemption through Christ. While Christians are not under the Mosaic law for salvation, it provides timeless moral principles that guide believers in righteous living. The principles found in the law offer practical guidance in addressing various life challenges and ethical dilemmas. The law helps individuals understand God's standard of righteousness, leading to a deeper appreciation of God's grace and mercy.

It points to Christ because our inability to justify ourselves by keeping the law emphasizes the necessity of faith in Christ for salvation. While Christians are not saved by keeping the law, obedience to God's moral principles is an expression of love and devotion to Him.

By integrating the right understanding of the law into biblical counseling, counselors can help individuals grasp the significance of God's standard, recognize their need for grace, and embrace a life of obedience motivated by love for God. The law serves as a reminder of our need for a Savior and points us to Christ as the ultimate fulfillment of God's righteous requirements.

Redemption through Christ

Redemption through Christ is at the heart of biblical counseling. It is the central message of the gospel, emphasizing that through Jesus Christ's sacrificial death and resurrection, humankind can find forgiveness of sins and restoration of a right relationship with God. "In [Jesus] we have redemption through his blood, the forgiveness of sins, according to the riches of his grace" (Eph 1:7). Our redemption is through the blood of Christ, and it is by God's grace that our sins are forgiven. Justification, or being declared righteous before God, is made possible through the redemption found in Christ Jesus. Paul explains that believers are "justified freely by his grace through the redemption that is in Christ Jesus" (Rom 3:24) because God "hath delivered us from the power of darkness, and hath translated us into the kingdom of his dear Son: In whom we have redemption through his blood, even the forgiveness of sins" (Col 1:13–14).

Redemption through Christ may be seen by some as merely a religious belief or a metaphorical concept, not means of personal salvation, but the biblical understanding of redemption through Christ is crucial for effective counseling. The message of redemption brings hope and healing to individuals struggling with guilt, shame, and brokenness, assuring them of God's love and forgiveness. It emphasizes the need for genuine repentance and faith in Christ as the way to find forgiveness and restoration. Guiding individuals toward a deeper relationship with Christ leads to lasting transformation and growth. Grasping the concept of redemption helps counselees understand their true identity as redeemed children of God who finding their worth in Christ alone. It also encourages individuals to extend forgiveness to others as they themselves have been forgiven through Christ's sacrifice. This gives people an eternal perspective, reminding them of the hope of everlasting life through Christ and providing comfort and strength in times of difficulty.

By integrating the understanding of redemption through Christ into biblical counseling, counselors can lead individuals to experience the life-changing power of God's love and grace. This approach fosters spiritual growth, emotional healing, and a deep sense of purpose and belonging in Christ. It serves as the foundation for transformation and renewal in the lives of those seeking guidance and counsel.

Justification and Sanctification

Justification and sanctification are important theological concepts in biblical counseling, representing distinct but interconnected aspects of a believer's journey with God.

Justification is the act of God declaring a sinner righteous through faith in Jesus Christ, apart from any human effort or adherence to the law. "Therefore we conclude that a man is justified by faith without the deeds of the law" (Rom 3:28). "Therefore being justified by faith, we have peace with God through our Lord Jesus Christ" (Rom 5:1) Through faith in Christ, believers are justified and experience reconciliation with God, receiving peace and assurance of salvation.

Sanctification refers to being set apart and made holy by God through an ongoing process of growth in godly character and conduct. "This is the will of God, even your sanctification, that ye should abstain from fornication" (1 Thess 4:3).

As Paul prayed for the Thessalonian believers, "[May] the very God of peace sanctify you wholly; and I pray God your whole spirit and soul and body be preserved blameless unto the coming of our Lord Jesus Christ" (1 Thess 5:23). Sanctification encompasses the complete transformation of a believer, involving his spirit, soul, and body, resulting in blamelessness in Christ.

Understanding justification and sanctification is crucial in biblical counseling for several reasons. First of all, it is necessary for counselees to have assurance of salvation. The basis for that is emphasizing that justification is by faith in Christ alone, affirming their salvation and security in Him. This understanding encourages repentance and faith. Biblical counselors guide individuals to place their faith in Christ for justification and lead them to repentance for sanctification. It also promotes spiritual growth by assisting believers in their journey of sanctification through spiritual disciplines in reliance on the Holy Spirit. The counselor should emphasize that justification and sanctification are gifts of God's grace, underscoring the believer's dependence on Him. Biblical counseling Integrates faith and life by helping individuals apply biblical principles to their daily lives, aligning their thoughts and actions with God's Word. The outcome is that individuals can become more like Christ through the process of sanctification, reflecting His character and love.

By integrating the understanding of justification and sanctification into biblical counseling, counselors can help believers grow in their faith, embrace their identity in Christ, and experience transformation by the power of the Holy Spirit. This provides a comprehensive framework for spiritual development and guides individuals toward a deeper and more meaningful relationship with God.

The Role of the Holy Spirit

The Holy Spirit plays a vital role in biblical counseling, as highlighted throughout the Scriptures. As the third person of the Trinity, the Holy Spirit is actively involved in the lives of believers—guiding, empowering, and transforming them.

Jesus promised His followers, "The Comforter, which is the Holy Ghost, whom the Father will send in my name, he shall teach you all things, and bring all things to your remembrance, whatsoever I have said unto you" (John 14:26). The Holy Spirit is the Comforter sent by the Father, and He is the teacher who guides believers into truth and enables them to recall the teachings of Jesus. Paul wrote, "Likewise the Spirit also helpeth our infirmities: for we know not what we should pray for as we ought: but the Spirit itself maketh intercession for us with groanings which cannot be uttered" (Rom 8:26). The Holy Spirit helps believers in their weaknesses, even in prayer, interceding on their behalf before God. "The fruit of the Spirit is love, joy, peace, longsuffering, gentleness, goodness, faith, meekness, temperance: against such there is no law" (Gal 5:22–23). The Holy Spirit produces godly character qualities in the lives of believers, leading to transformation and conformity to Christ's image.

Understanding the role of the Holy Spirit is essential in biblical counseling for the following reasons. The Spirit is the ultimate guide in counseling sessions, leading both the counselor and the counselee toward truth and wisdom. He is also the source of strength, comfort, and peace for the believer during challenging life circumstances. We must further understand that the Holy Spirit convicts individuals of sin, leading them to repentance and transformation. We rely on Him for spiritual growth so we can bear fruit and live according to God's will. It is important to trusting in the Holy Spirit's intercession, particularly when we do not know how to express our deepest needs. The Holy Spirit can work through the counseling process to bring about healing, restoration, and change in the lives of counselees.

By integrating this understanding of the role of the Holy Spirit in biblical counseling, counselors can invite the presence and guidance of the Spirit into their sessions. This approach fosters a deeper sense of reliance on God's wisdom and power, leading to more transformative and spiritually impactful counseling experiences. It acknowledges that true change and healing come from the work of the Holy Spirit in the hearts and lives of those seeking counsel.

God's Grace and Mercy

The grace and mercy of the Lord are foundational principles in biblical counseling, highlighting His unmerited favor and compassion towards humanity. Salvation is a result of God's grace, a gift freely given through faith in Jesus Christ, not earned through human effort or works. "By grace are ye saved through faith; and that not of yourselves: it is the gift of God: not of works, lest any man should boast" (Eph 2:8–9). "It is of the LORD's mercies that we are not consumed because his compassions fail not. They are new every morning: great is thy faithfulness" (Lam 3:22–23). God's mercies are abundant and fresh every single day, demonstrating His unwavering compassion and faithfulness towards His people. Despite human sinfulness, God's grace abounds even more, offering forgiveness and reconciliation through Christ. "Where sin abounded, grace did much more abound" (Rom 5:20).

The concepts of grace and mercy may be viewed as simply acts of kindness, compassion, and forgiveness, but not necessarily tied to a divine source. In biblical counseling, however, a proper understanding of God as the giver of grace and mercy is essential. Communicating God's grace and mercy provide hope and healing to those burdened by sin, guilt, and shame. The biblical counselor should emphasize that God's unconditional love is not based on human performance but on His character of grace and mercy and that God stands ready to forgive those who genuinely repent and seek Him.

In light of God's compassion, counselors ought to demonstrate grace and mercy toward counselees, reflecting God's character in their interactions. Rightly understanding divine grace and mercy will help individuals realize that they are valued and loved by God despite their past sinful choices and shortcomings. This approach encourages spiritual growth, guiding individuals to respond to God's grace by growing in faith, love, and obedience to Him.

By integrating this biblical understanding of God's grace and mercy into their counseling, counselors can create a safe and accepting environment where individuals can experience God's love, forgiveness, and transformation. It fosters a deep sense of gratitude for and awe of God's character, drawing individuals closer to Him and inspiring them to extend grace and mercy to others in their journey of healing and growth.

Identity in Christ

Since "if any man be in Christ, he is a new creature: old things are passed away; behold, all things are become new" (2 Cor 5:17), identity in Christ is a fundamental concept in biblical counseling, emphasizing how believers' true identity is found in their relationship with Jesus Christ. As Paul put it, "I am crucified with Christ: nevertheless I live; yet not I, but Christ liveth in me: and the life which I now live in the flesh I live by the faith of the Son of God, who loved me, and gave himself for me" (Gal 2:20). Believers experience a profound spiritual union with Christ in which He lives in them and becomes the source of their new life. "Ye are a chosen generation, a royal priesthood, an holy nation, a peculiar people; that ye should shew forth the praises of him who hath called you out of darkness into his marvellous light" (1 Pet 2:9). This is believers' unique and significant identity in Christ.

Psychology sees identity as being shaped by personal experiences, relationships, and cultural influences without any spiritual or religious dimension. By contrast, biblical counseling sees a scriptural concept of identity in Christ as essential for helping counselees (a) to recognize their value and worth as beloved children of God, regardless of their past mistakes or societal labels, and (b) to find their self-esteem in Christ's love and acceptance rather than seeking validation from external sources.

This is the basis for encouraging individuals to reject negative self-perceptions and embrace their identity as new creations in Christ, empowered by the Holy Spirit to grow in godly character. Through understanding their identity in Christ, individuals can experience emotional healing and restoration from past hurts and discover their purpose and calling in life as people chosen and loved by God.

Biblical counselors can help individuals experience a profound sense of purpose, acceptance, and belonging by integrating the understanding of identity in Christ into their counseling. This provides a solid foundation for emotional healing, personal growth, and spiritual transformation. Understanding your identity in Christ empowers you to live a life that reflects God's love and grace, impacting every aspect of your being and relationships.

Overcoming Shame and Regret

Shame and regret are common emotions experienced by individuals due to past mistakes, failures, or sins. These emotions are addressed in biblical counseling by giving the counselee the hope of finding healing, forgiveness, and restoration.

The promises of God's Word (e.g., 1 John 1:9 "If we confess our sins, he is faithful and just to forgive us our sins, and to cleanse us from all unrighteousness") are the basis for offering freedom from shame and guilt to counselees who genuinely confess their sins to God. The psalmist knew that turning to God and seeking His forgiveness brings relief and lightens the burden of shame: "They looked unto him, and were lightened: and their faces were not ashamed" (Ps 34:5). And so did the prophet Isaiah: "Come now, and let us reason together, saith the LORD: though your sins be as scarlet, they shall be as white as snow; though they be red like crimson, they shall be as wool" (Isa 1:18). God promises to wash away our sins, making us clean and free from the stain of shame.

Psychologists often address shame and regret with techniques focused on self-compassion, self-forgiveness, and self-acceptance, approaches that draw on cognitive and behavioral strategies. Biblical counseling considers shame and regret spiritual issues, guiding individuals to confess their sins to God, genuinely repent, and experience His forgiveness. Emphasizing that God's grace is greater than any sin or regret and that His mercy is available to all who seek Him creates a safe space for individuals to express their feelings of shame and regret without judgment. Biblical counselors offer healing by pointing individuals to Jesus Christ, the only one who can provide healing, restoration, and freedom from shame. People will grow in their relationship with God as they find their security and identity in Him rather than in past mistakes.

By integrating the biblical perspective on shame and regret, counselors can help individuals experience the transformative power of God's forgiveness and grace. This approach fosters emotional healing, reconciliation with God, and a renewed sense of purpose and hope. Understanding that God's love is greater than our failures allows individuals to let go of shame and regret and embrace a life filled with His peace and joy.

Renewing the Mind

The renewal of the mind is a crucial aspect of biblical counseling, highlighting the transformation of one's thoughts and beliefs through the power of God's Word and the Holy Spirit as set forth by the apostle Paul: "Be not conformed to this world: but be ye transformed by the renewing of your mind, that ye may prove what is that good, and acceptable, and perfect, will of God" (Rom 12:2); "be renewed in the spirit of your mind" (Eph 4:23); and "put on the new man, which is renewed in knowledge after the image of him that created him" (Col 3:10). Believers are called to resist the patterns of the world and undergo a transformation by renewing their minds according to God's will. Renewal of the mind is a continuous process as we allow the Holy Spirit to transform our thinking and attitudes. Through this process, believers take on a new nature that reflects the character of Christ, acquired through knowledge of Him.

Renewing the mind may be viewed as a psychological process of changing negative thought patterns and behaviors, often through cognitive-behavioral therapy or other counseling techniques, but the biblical concept of renewing the mind is foundational in biblical counseling.

Negative thought patterns can be transformed as individuals learn to replace destructive ideation with biblical truths. Counselors help by guiding individuals to align their beliefs and values with the truths found in God's Word. Addressing deeply ingrained patterns of thinking that hinder spiritual growth and emotional healing can help overcome strongholds. As counselees engage in regular study and meditation on Scripture to renew their minds, they can develop a strong foundation of faith, trusting in God's promises and character. An essential part of the biblical counselor's job is to encourage individuals to grow in their relationship with God by allowing His Spirit to transform their minds.

When counselors integrate the correct understanding of renewing the mind into their counseling, it can help individuals experience significant changes in their thoughts, attitudes, and behaviors. This approach fosters spiritual growth, emotional healing, and a deeper relationship with God. Through the power of the Holy Spirit and the truths found in God's Word, individuals can experience freedom from destructive thought patterns and live in accordance with God's good, acceptable, and perfect will.

Coping with Temptation

"There hath no temptation taken you but such as is common to man: but God is faithful, who will not suffer you to be tempted above that ye are able; but will with the temptation also make a way to escape, that ye may be able to bear it" (1 Cor 10:13). Temptation is an everyday struggle faced by individuals, and biblical counseling addresses the importance of relying on God's strength and wisdom to resist and overcome it. God promises to provide a way out: "Submit yourselves therefore to God. Resist the devil, and he will flee from you" (James 4:7). Memorizing and meditating on God's Word helps individuals combat temptation by filling their hearts and minds with His truth. "Thy word have I hid in mine heart, that I might not sin against thee" (Ps 119:11).

From a secular perspective, dealing with temptation may be seen as a matter of employing various strategies such as cognitive reframing, self-control techniques, and mindfulness practices to resist unhealthy urges. For Christians, understanding how to resist temptation biblically is integral to effective counseling. A biblical counselor will encourage individuals to depend on God's strength and guidance when faced with temptation and to have accountability partners or support systems to help them apply biblical principles to their specific areas of struggle and temptation. Biblical counselors also encourage counselees to develop prayer habits, especially to seek God's help and guidance when dealing with temptations. These counselors will also highlight the Holy Spirit's work in empowering believers to live victoriously over temptation. At the same time, they will reminding counselees that everyone faces temptations and it's all right to seek forgiveness when they fall short.

By integrating the understanding of coping with temptation into their counseling, biblical counselors can provide individuals with effective tools and spiritual strategies to overcome temptation and grow in their faith. This approach fosters spiritual resilience, maturity, and a deeper reliance on God's grace and strength to lead a life pleasing to Him. Ultimately, counseling individuals on how to cope with temptation aligns with the biblical goal of pursuing holiness and honoring God in all aspects of life.

Extending Grace to Others

Extending grace to others is a core principle of biblical counseling, rooted in God's example of showing grace and forgiveness to humanity. A solid scriptural foundation supports this practice:

- Ephesians 4:32 says, "Be ye kind one to another, tenderhearted, forgiving one another, even as God for Christ's sake hath forgiven you." This verse encourages believers to be kind and compassionate, following God's example of extending grace by forgiving offenses.

- Colossians 3:13 requires "forbearing" and "forgiving" each other. "If any man have a quarrel against any: even as Christ forgave you, so also do ye." So just as Christ forgave us, we are called to forgive others, demonstrating grace and mercy in our relationships.

- Luke 6:37 records the words of Jesus: "Judge not, and ye shall not be judged: condemn not, and ye shall not be condemned: forgive, and ye shall be forgiven." This emphasizes the importance of not judging or condemning others, but choosing to extend forgiveness and grace instead.

Giving grace to others is a compassionate and sympathetic response to human imperfections and shortcomings, flowing from our own experience of receiving the forgiveness of the Lord. This is a key concept in biblical counseling. Encouraging individuals to extend grace and forgiveness in their relationships promotes reconciliation and harmony and helps them heal from past hurts and offenses, guiding them toward forgiveness and freedom from bitterness. Demonstrating Christlike love by showing grace to others facilitates conflict resolution. Biblical counselors remind individuals about God's abundant mercy toward them, encouraging them to extend the same to others. This helps counselees experience emotional healing and spiritual growth.

Counseling that incorporates the importance of extending grace to others promotes healing, reconciliation, and spiritual transformation. This approach fosters humility, compassion, and a deeper sense of unity among believers, reflecting God's love and grace in their interactions. It empowers individuals to break free from the chains of unforgiveness and bitterness, embracing a life of love, forgiveness, and grace.

Healing from Past Wounds

Healing from past wounds is a significant aspect of biblical counseling, through which individuals find restoration and comfort in God's love and grace. "He healeth the broken in heart, and bindeth up their wounds" (Ps 147:3). God is the ultimate healer, comforting those with broken hearts and easing the pain of their emotional wounds. Isaiah proclaimed, "The Spirit of the Lord God is upon me; because the Lord hath anointed me to preach good tidings unto the meek; he hath sent me to bind up the brokenhearted, to proclaim liberty to the captives, and the opening of the prison to them that are bound" (Isa 61:1). This pointed to the future ministry of Jesus, who brings healing to the brokenhearted and sets captives free from emotional and spiritual bondage. When Jesus came, He gave this invitation: "Come unto me, all ye that labour and are heavy laden, and I will give you rest. Take my yoke upon you, and learn of me; for I am meek and lowly in heart: and ye shall find rest unto your souls. For my yoke is easy, and my burden is light" (Matt 11:28–30). Inviting those burdened by past wounds to find rest in Him, He promised comfort and relief from their troubles.

Our culture's method of healing past wounds may involve various therapeutic approaches aimed at processing and resolving emotional pain, such as trauma-focused therapy or other cognitive behavioral techniques. From a biblical worldview perspective, counselees need to know that God is the source of true emotional and spiritual healing and that forgiveness is the way to release the burden of past hurts. Using Scripture to bring comfort and encouragement helps people find hope in God's promises. Lasting healing comes through identifying and addressing root causes of past wounds. Biblical counselors encourage vulnerability by creating a safe and supportive environment for counselees to open up about their past wounds and traumas. It is also important to recognize that healing from past wounds is a journey that requires trust and patience in God's timing.

By integrating the biblical understanding of healing from past wounds into their counseling, counselors can walk alongside individuals as they experience emotional and spiritual restoration. This approach empowers individuals to find healing, peace, and strength in God's love, allowing them to move forward with renewed hope and resilience. Embracing God's healing grace, individuals can leave their past wounds behind and step into a future filled with His abundant love and purpose.

Living a Spirit-Filled Life

Living a Spirit-filled life is a vital aspect of biblical counseling, emphasizing the significance of relying on the Holy Spirit for guidance, empowerment, and transformation. "Be not drunk with wine, wherein is excess; but be filled with the Spirit" (Eph 5:18). Believers are encouraged to be continually filled with the Holy Spirit, allowing His presence and power to control their lives.

Galatians 5:16 contains a command and a promise: "Walk in the Spirit, and ye shall not fulfil the lust of the flesh." Walking in the Spirit means living in obedience to God's Word, which enables believers to overcome sinful desires: "For they that are after the flesh do mind the things of the flesh; but they that are after the Spirit the things of the Spirit. For to be carnally minded is death; but to be spiritually minded is life and peace" (Rom 8:5–6). Being filled with the Spirit brings life and peace, while focusing on worldly desires leads to spiritual death.

Understanding how to live a Spirit-filled life is essential in biblical counseling. Biblical counselors teach their counselees to depend on the Holy Spirit for wisdom, discernment, and strength and to align their lives with God's Word so the Spirit can transform their character. Counselees are encouraged to discern God's will through prayer and listening to the Holy Spirit's leading through Scripture. Biblical counseling helps individuals to resist temptation and walk in the Spirit's power to live victoriously over sin. As they grow spiritually, they manifest the fruit of the Spirit (love, joy, peace, patience, kindness, goodness, faithfulness, gentleness, and self-control) in their lives. Counselees receive guidance in how to deepen their relationship with God through prayer, worship, and studying His Word.

The biblical counselor integrates the understanding of living a Spirit-filled life into counseling to help individuals experience a closer walk with God, resulting in a life characterized by love, joy, peace, and spiritual growth. This approach empowers individuals to face life's challenges with confidence, knowing that they are not alone but have the indwelling presence of the Holy Spirit to guide and empower them. Living a Spirit-filled life leads to greater alignment with God's design and a deeper sense of purpose, fulfillment, and peace in one's journey of faith.

Cultivating Repentant Hearts

Cultivating a repentant heart is a foundational aspect of life change in biblical counseling, emphasizing the significance of genuine sorrow for sin and turning toward God in humility and obedience. In his day, Peter preached to unbelievers, "Repent ye therefore, and be converted, that your sins may be blotted out when the times of refreshing shall come from the presence of the Lord." The call to repentance promises forgiveness and refreshment from the Lord for those who turn away from sin.

"Godly sorrow worketh repentance to salvation not to be repented of: but the sorrow of the world worketh death" (2 Cor 7:10). The kind of sorrow that leads to genuine repentance is called "godly sorrow," and it leads to salvation and spiritual transformation, while worldly sorrow brings spiritual death. Jesus said, "I came not to call the righteous, but sinners to repentance" (Luke 5:32). By calling sinners to repentance, He showed the importance of turning away from sin and embracing God's forgiveness.

Cultivating repentant hearts involves encouraging individuals to take responsibility for their actions, make amends, and seek personal growth and change. Understanding what it means to have a repentant heart is a vital part of biblical counseling. The counselor should assist individuals to recognize and acknowledge their sins and their need for forgiveness. As they experience godly sorrow for their sins, leading to heartfelt repentance, they should seek forgiveness from God and others they may have hurt.

The effective counselor will encourage individuals to take appropriate steps to make amends for their actions and seek reconciliation, turning to God in humility and seeking His guidance and transforming power. Counselees should focus on God's abundant grace and mercy for those who genuinely repent.

Biblical counselors who inculcate this understanding of cultivating a repentant heart can help counselees experience true transformation and spiritual growth. This approach empowers individuals to find freedom from guilt and shame through God's forgiveness, leading to a deeper relationship with Him. Cultivating repentant hearts fosters humility, brokenness, and a genuine desire to live in obedience to God's will, resulting in a life that honors and pleases Him.

Embracing the Journey of Redemption

Embracing the journey of redemption is a central theme in biblical counseling, highlighting the transformative power of God's grace and the restoration of broken lives. God promises to forgive and redeem His people, inviting them to return to Him for restoration: "I have blotted out, as a thick cloud, thy transgressions, and, as a cloud, thy sins: return unto me; for I have redeemed thee" (Isa 44:2). The psalmist acknowledges God's abundant redemption and mercy, assuring believers of His willingness to redeem them from their sins: "Let Israel hope in the Lord: for with the Lord there is mercy, and with him is plenteous redemption. And he shall redeem Israel from all his iniquities" (Ps 130:7–8). Ephesians 1:7 says, "In [Christ] we have redemption through his blood, the forgiveness of sins, according to the riches of his grace." Redemption is made possible through the sacrificial blood of Jesus, which provides forgiveness and reconciles believers with God.

Psychologists may talk about a process of personal growth and transformation, often involving therapy or self-improvement strategies, but in biblical counseling embracing the journey of redemption is essential because counselees must do the following in order to change:

- Acknowledge their brokenness and need for redemption
- Accept God's grace and boundless love, which brings redemption through Jesus Christ

- Activate their hope based on God's willingness to redeem and restore their lives

- Heal past wounds and hurts through the redemptive power of God's forgiveness

- Pursue spiritual growth and maturity as they embrace God's redemptive work

- Ground their identity in Christ, recognizing that their worth and value come from being redeemed by Him

As biblical counselors embrace this understanding of the journey of redemption and integrate it into their counseling, they can provide a framework for individuals to experience God's transformative grace. This approach empowers counselees to move forward from their past mistakes, wounds, and regrets, embracing a life marked by redemption, forgiveness, and hope. Embracing the journey of redemption leads to a deeper relationship with God and a greater understanding of His redemptive plan for each person's life.

> **Do you understand everything you have read in this chapter?**
> If not, please read it again before moving on to Chapter 4.

CHAPTER 4

Mistakes in Biblical Counseling

In life's trials, we discover the importance of putting our trust in God's control and finding comfort in His purposes.

Mistakes made in biblical counseling have various implications for both the counselor and the counselee. Here are some common mistakes that can occur in the course of a counseling session:

- **Overreliance on Personal Opinions:** One mistake biblical counselors sometimes make is relying solely on their personal opinions or experiences rather than seeking guidance from God's Word. Counselors must be diligent in ensuring that their advice aligns with biblical principles.

- **Lack of Cultural Sensitivity:** Failing to consider the cultural background, beliefs, and practices of the counselee can lead to misunderstandings and ineffective counseling. Biblical counselors should be sensitive to and respectful of diverse cultural perspectives.

- **Judgmental Attitude:** Being judgmental or condemning toward counselees for their struggles or mistakes can hinder the counseling process. Instead, counselors should demonstrate compassion and unconditional love, just as Christ does.

- **Ignoring Underlying Mental Health Issues:** Mistakes can occur when biblical counselors overlook or dismiss underlying mental health issues. It is crucial to recognize when professional mental health intervention is needed and make appropriate referrals.

- **Insufficient Knowledge of Scripture:** Inadequate understanding of God's Word can lead to misinterpretations or improper applications of biblical principles. Biblical counselors should continually seek to deepen their knowledge of Scripture.

- **Imposing Solutions:** Forcing a particular solution or approach on the counselee without considering the individual's needs and circumstances can be counterproductive. Biblical counseling should focus on guiding the counselee toward discovering God's will for his or her life.

- **Ineffective Communication:** Poor communication skills can lead to misunderstandings, frustration, and a lack of progress in the counseling relationship. Biblical counselors should strive for clarity and practice active listening.

- **Emotional Overinvolvement:** Allowing personal emotions or biases to affect the counseling process can hinder objectivity and compromise the counselee's best interests. Counselors should maintain appropriate professional boundaries.

- **Unrealistic Expectations:** Expecting immediate or total change can lead to disappointment and discouragement. Biblical counseling is a gradual process, and growth takes time.

- **Neglecting Self-Care:** A counselor's failure to prioritize self-care can result in burnout and reduced effectiveness. It is essential for counselors to maintain their own emotional, physical, and spiritual well-being.

It is important to acknowledge that counselors, like anyone, can make mistakes. However, recognizing and learning from these mistakes can lead to personal and professional growth, improving the quality of future counseling interactions. Biblical counselors should continually seek God's guidance, remain humble, and rely on the Holy Spirit to guide them in their role as instruments of God's love and healing.

Now let's look at each category in detail.

Overreliance on Personal Opinions

It is problematic when the counselor places undue emphasis on his or her own thoughts, beliefs, and experiences rather than seeking guidance from God's Word and the leading of the Holy Spirit. The Bible warns against leaning solely on human understanding and encourages seeking wisdom from God: "Trust in the Lord with all thine heart; and lean not unto thine own understanding. In all thy ways acknowledge him, and he shall direct thy paths" (Prov 3:5–6). In biblical counseling, counselors should acknowledge the sufficiency of God's wisdom and seek His direction for counseling decisions. "My thoughts are not your thoughts, neither are your ways my ways, saith the Lord. For as the heavens are higher than the earth, so are my ways higher than your ways, and my thoughts than your thoughts" (Isa 55:8–9). Overreliance on personal opinions can lead to limited perspectives, but God's thoughts and ways are higher and wiser. Biblical counselors must recognize the need to align their counseling with God's truth and not merely rely on their own limited understanding.

Counselors' tendency to prioritize their own beliefs, biases, or preferences over evidence-based practices or objective guidance may stem from their own subjective experiences or worldview, which could hinder the effectiveness of counseling interventions. Overreliance on personal opinions in counseling can result in several harmful effects.

1. Confirmation bias: Counselors may unconsciously favor information or interpretations that align with their preexisting beliefs, while dismissing or ignoring contrary evidence.

2. Limited perspective: Relying solely on personal opinions may result in overlooking alternative viewpoints or approaches that could benefit the counselee.

3. Lack of flexibility: A counselor who overly depends on his own opinions may resist adapting his or her approach to better fit the unique needs and circumstances of the counselee.

4. Lack of objectivity: Overreliance on personal opinions can compromise the counselor's objectivity in understanding the counselee's situation and providing appropriate guidance.

5. Inconsistent advice: The counselor may provide inconsistent or conflicting advice based on personal biases, which can confuse the counselee and hinder progress.

A better approach is to balance personal insights with biblical truth. From both the biblical and secular perspectives, it is essential for counselors to recognize the potential pitfalls of overreliance on personal opinions. Instead, counselors should strive to integrate their personal insights and experiences with biblical truths, prayerful consideration, and evidence-based practices. Biblical counselors must continuously seek God's guidance and align their counseling with His Word. In doing so, they can provide counseling that reflects God's wisdom and love, transcending their limited understanding and bringing hope, healing, and transformation to those they serve.

Lack of Cultural Sensitivity

The Bible emphasizes the value of cultural sensitivity in the way we relate to and treat others. It teaches us to love our neighbors as ourselves and to show respect and compassion to people from all walks of life, regardless of their cultural background.

"There is neither Jew nor Greek, there is neither bond nor free, there is neither male nor female: for ye are all one in Christ Jesus" (Gal 3:28). This verse emphasizes the equality and unity of believers in Christ, irrespective of their cultural or social distinctions. A parallel passage teaches that in Christ, cultural differences should not divide or marginalize people: "There is neither Greek nor Jew, circumcision nor uncircumcision, Barbarian, Scythian, bond nor free: but Christ is all, and in all" (Col 3:11). Biblical counseling should be free from any form of discrimination or bias. Biblical counselors are called to embrace and understand the diverse cultural backgrounds of the counselees they serve.

In a secular context, lack of cultural sensitivity in counseling refers to the failure to recognize and respect the unique cultural values, beliefs, norms, and practices of counselees. It involves overlooking or misunderstanding the impact of culture on the counselee's worldview and experiences.

The absence of cultural sensitivity is evident in a variety of counseling behaviors or attitudes including (1) ethnocentrism (unconsciously imposing your own cultural values and assumptions onto the counselee without considering the counselee's cultural context), (2) stereotyping (making assumptions about the counselee based on cultural overgeneralizations), (3) insensitivity to religious beliefs (failing to understand and respect the counselee's faith commitments and practices), (4) language barriers (inability to communicate effectively due to linguistic differences), and (5) misinterpreting behaviors or emotions displayed by the counselee,

From either the biblical or the secular perspective, cultural sensitivity is essential in providing effective and compassionate counseling. Here are some key considerations for integrating cultural sensitivity with biblical principles:

- **Respect and Sympathy:** Biblical counselors should approach all their counselees with respect, compassion, and a willingness to try to understand their cultural context.

- **Cross-Cultural Awareness:** Counselors should educate themselves about the cultural backgrounds of the counselees they serve, seeking to understand how cultural factors may impact their experiences and perspectives.

- **Open Dialogue:** Encourage uninhibited dialogue with counselees, allowing them to share their cultural beliefs, values, and experiences without judgment.

- **Language Access:** If language barriers exist, consider utilizing interpreters or other resources to facilitate effective communication.

- **Tailored Approach:** Flexibly adapt counseling techniques and interventions to be culturally relevant and sensitive to the individual needs of the counselee.

By embracing cultural sensitivity in their counseling, biblical counselors can foster a safe and inclusive environment where counselees feel heard, respected, and supported in their journey towards healing and growth. On the other hand, failing to consider the cultural background, beliefs, and practices of the counselee can lead to misunderstandings and ineffective counseling. Biblical counselors should be sensitive to and respectful of diverse cultural perspectives.

Judgmental Attitude

A judgmental attitude in counseling refers to a critical or condemning approach to the counselee. It is contrary to the biblical teachings on showing love, grace, and mercy to others, as Christ demonstrated during His ministry: "Judge not, that ye be not judged. For with what judgment ye judge, ye shall be judged: and with what measure ye mete, it shall be measured to you again" (Matt 7:1–2). Jesus cautions about judging others because we will be judged by the same standard we use. In contrast, biblical counseling should embody a spirit of compassion and understanding. "Judge not, and ye shall not be judged: condemn not, and ye shall not be condemned: forgive, and ye shall be forgiven" (Luke 6:37). This verse reinforces the importance of not condemning others, but rather extending forgiveness and grace. In biblical counseling, counselors should aim to provide a nonjudgmental and forgiving atmosphere. A judgmental attitude lacks the spirit of meekness and humility required to help restore a fallen brother or sister. Biblical counselors should approach the counselee with gentleness and understanding. "Brethren, if a man be overtaken in a fault, ye which are spiritual, restore such an one in the spirit of meekness; considering thyself, lest thou also be tempted" (Gal 6:1).

In secular terms, a judgmental attitude in counseling refers to the counselor's inclination to pass harsh or critical judgments on the counselee's thoughts, behaviors, or experiences, which obviously negatively impacts the counseling relationship by making the counselee feel rejected or misunderstood. Such a mindset on the part of the counselor may be reflected in several ways: (1) criticizing the counselee's past choices or decisions, rather than seeking to understand the underlying reasons and providing guidance for change, (2) imposing your own moral values and beliefs on the counselee without considering the counselee's individual circumstances, (3) showing a lack of compassion, which makes the counselee feel judged or unworthy, or (4) using a condescending tone of voice that undermines the counselee's self-esteem and openness.

Both biblical and secular counseling perspectives emphasize the importance of avoiding a judgmental attitude. Instead, counselors should foster an atmosphere of grace, understanding, and acceptance. For that to happen, biblical counselors need to develop three qualities:

- **Compassion:** Cultivate sympathy for the counselee's struggles and challenges, recognizing that everyone faces difficulties.

- **Active Listening:** Actively listen to the counselee's experiences without passing judgment, showing genuine concern.

- **Humility:** Maintain a meek attitude, acknowledging that each person is on his or her own journey and needs God's grace.

A redemptive approach focuses on restoration and growth rather than condemnation, helping the counselee move forward positively. By embodying a nonjudgmental and compassionate attitude, biblical counselors can create a safe and supportive environment, allowing the counselee to open up and engage in the counseling process with trust and hope for healing and transformation. Being judgmental or condemning toward the counselee for their struggles or past mistakes will hinder the counseling process. Instead, counselors should demonstrate acceptance and unconditional love, just as Christ does.

Chapter 4

Ignoring Underlying Mental Health Issues

Ignoring underlying mental health issues in biblical counseling involves the failure to recognize and address psychological conditions that may be contributing to the counselee's struggles. This can happen when counselors attribute psychological distress solely to spiritual causes and overlook the potential coexistence of mental health challenges.

The Bible acknowledges the spiritual aspect of human beings but also recognizes the complexities of the human mind and emotions as well as the physical body. While faith and spiritual growth are vital in biblical counseling, the Bible also emphasizes the importance of addressing emotional pain and brokenness. Here are a few examples:

- **Psalm 34:18** "The Lord is nigh unto them that are of a broken heart; and saveth such as be of a contrite spirit." The Bible acknowledges emotional distress and brokenness, highlighting God's closeness to those who are hurting. In biblical counseling, it is essential to recognize and address emotional struggles with sensitivity and understanding.

- **Proverbs 12:25** "Heaviness in the heart of man maketh it stoop: but a good word maketh it glad." This verse mentions the impact of emotional distress on a person's well-being. Biblical counselors should be attentive to signs of emotional distress and offer appropriate support and encouragement.

- **Isaiah 61:1** "The Spirit of the Lord God is upon me; because the Lord hath anointed me to preach good tidings unto the meek; he hath sent me to bind up the brokenhearted, to proclaim liberty to the captives, and the opening of the prison to them that are bound." In light of God's concern for those who are brokenhearted and in emotional captivity, biblical counselors should follow His example by dealing with emotional pain and helping to heal the wounds of the brokenhearted.

The failure to recognize and address diagnosable mental health conditions often stems from a lack of training or understanding of mental health matters and may involve the following:

1. Inadequate assessment—not conducting a thorough evaluation to identify potential mental health conditions and their impact on the counselee's well-being

2. Minimizing symptoms—downplaying or dismissing the significance of emotional distress, which can prevent the counselee from receiving appropriate care

3. Misattributing symptoms—assuming that all emotional struggles are solely the result of spiritual issues, without considering the possibility of mental health conditions

4. Lack of referral—not referring the counselee to a qualified mental health professional when necessary, especially when symptoms are severe or persistent

In both the biblical and secular approaches, it is essential for counselors to recognize the potential coexistence of spiritual and mental health issues. Instead of ignoring or dismissing mental health concerns, biblical counselors can integrate spiritual and mental health approaches to provide comprehensive care by working in collaboration with mental health professionals to address both spiritual and psychological needs. Adopting a more holistic approach, counselors should acknowledge the interconnectedness of the mind, body, and spirit, understanding that emotional struggles may have multifaceted causes. By demonstrating compassion and understanding of counselees, they can provide a safe space for them to share their emotions and experiences. Finally, they should be willing to refer the counselee to a qualified mental health professional for further evaluation and treatment, especially when mental health conditions are suspected.

Through integrating spiritual and mental health approaches, biblical counselors can offer a more comprehensive and effective counseling experience, addressing the whole person and promoting healing and growth in both spiritual and emotional dimensions.

Insufficient Knowledge of Scripture

Another mistake or problem in counseling is the counselor's lack of familiarity with or understanding of God's Word, which is essential for providing effective and accurate counsel. The Bible emphasizes the importance of knowing and applying Scripture in counseling situations.

"Study to shew thyself approved unto God, a workman that needeth not to be ashamed, rightly dividing the word of truth" Thus Paul urges believers to diligently study Scripture to be approved by God and to rightly handle the truth. In biblical counseling, counselors should strive to deepen their knowledge of Scripture to guide counselees with accuracy. Memorizing and internalizing God's Word will help you provide counsel rooted in biblical truth, enabling you to address counselees' struggles effectively. "Thy word have I hid in mine heart, that I might not sin against thee" (Ps 119:11).

As Hebrews 4:12 says, "The word of God is quick, and powerful, and sharper than any twoedged sword, piercing even to the dividing asunder of soul and spirit, and of the joints and marrow, and is a discerner of the thoughts and intents of the heart." Scripture is powerful and capable of penetrating the deepest parts of a person's being. Insufficient knowledge of Scripture can hinder the counselor's ability to discern and address the root issues of the counselee's heart.

Counselors who lack familiarity with the teachings and principles found in the Bible rely on personal opinions, secular ideologies, or other sources of guidance, neglecting the valuable insights and wisdom offered by the Bible. Specifically, this often results in the counselor (1) using minimal or inaccurate references to Scripture when providing counsel, (2) failing to integrate biblical teachings and principles into counseling sessions and relying more on secular approaches, and (3) struggling to apply God's Word effectively to the counselee's specific challenges.

To address the problem of insufficient knowledge of Scripture, counselors can take the following steps:

- **Continuous Study of God's Word:** Biblical counselors should commit to ongoing study and meditation on Scripture to deepen their understanding of God's teachings.

- **Training and Education:** Seeking formal training in biblical counseling and theology can enhance the counselor's knowledge and competence.

- **Seeking God's Guidance:** Rely on the guidance of the Holy Spirit to understand and apply Scripture appropriately in counseling situations.

- **Scriptural Integration:** Intentionally integrate biblical truths and principles into counseling sessions to provide counsel that aligns with God's Word.

Inadequate understanding of God's Word can lead to misinterpretations or improper application of biblical principles. By seeking to grow in biblical knowledge, biblical counselors can offer more informed and God-centered guidance, leading to more effective and transformative counseling experiences for their counselees.

Imposing Solutions

Counselors' inclination to force their own ideas, beliefs, or opinions on their counselees without considering each individual's unique circumstances and God's leading is another common mistake. The Bible emphasizes the importance of seeking divine guidance and allowing the Holy Spirit to work in the lives of both the counselor and the counselee: "Trust in the Lord with all thine heart; and lean not unto thine own understanding. In all thy ways acknowledge him, and he shall direct thy paths" (Prov 3:5–6). This passage encourages believers to trust in God rather than relying solely on their own mental capacity. In biblical counseling, counselors should avoid pressing counselees to accept their opinions and solutions but instead present God's wisdom in guiding the counselee. Biblical counselors should recognize that their solutions may not always align with God's perfect plan for the counselee. "For my thoughts are not your thoughts, neither are your ways my ways, saith the Lord. For as the heavens are higher than the earth, so are my ways higher than your ways, and my thoughts than your thoughts" (Isa 55:8–9). Rather than imposing worldly solutions, the biblical counsel will encourage the counselee to seek to be transformed by renewing his or her mind. "Be not conformed to this world: but be ye transformed by the renewing of your mind, that ye may prove what is that good, and acceptable, and perfect, will of God" (Rom 12:2).

In a secular context, counselors may tend to impose their preferred solutions or advice on the counselee without fully considering that individual's unique needs, preferences, and autonomy. This approach is client-centered and can hinder the counselee's growth and self-discovery. The biblical counselor should avoid applying a one-size-fits-all approach, offering the same solutions to all counselees regardless of their individual circumstances. If the counselor does not fully listen to the counselee's concerns and perspectives, it may lead to the imposition of solutions that do not resonate with the counselee. Failing to consider cultural differences or contextual factors that influence the counselee's preferences and choices may also be a problem. Both biblical and secular perspectives emphasize the importance of respecting the counselee's autonomy and uniqueness.

To avoid this error, biblical counselors can undertake the following four actions: (1) Seek God's guidance through prayer and rely on the Holy Spirit to discern the best approach for each counselee. (2) Listen carefully to the counselees' concerns, feelings, and perspectives, ensuring that their voice is heard and valued. (3) Adopt a client-centered approach that respects the counselee's autonomy, preferences, and values. (4) Facilitate the counselees' self-discovery process, helping them explore potential solutions and make informed decisions.

Forcing a particular solution or approach on counselees without considering their individual needs and circumstances can be counterproductive. Biblical counseling should focus on guiding counselees toward discovering God's will for their lives. By integrating God's will and a client-centered approach, biblical counselors can create a collaborative and supportive counseling environment where the counselees feel empowered to discover God's plan for their lives and find practical solutions that align with their faith and values.

Ineffective Communication

Ineffective communication in biblical counseling refers to a breakdown or lack of clear and meaningful communication between the counselor and the counselee. The Bible emphasizes the importance of using words wisely, speaking the truth in love, and fostering understanding and unity among believers. Gentle and respectful communication is powerful. In biblical counseling, counselors should strive to use soft words that can defuse tensions and promote constructive dialogue. "A soft answer turneth away wrath: but grievous words stir up anger" (Prov 15:1). The Bible encourages believers to use words that edify and minister grace to others. In biblical counseling, effective communication should aim to build up the counselees and promote their growth and healing. As Ephesians 4:29 says, "Let no corrupt communication proceed out of your mouth, but that which is good to the use of edifying, that it may minister grace unto the hearers." James offers this advice: "Wherefore, my beloved brethren, let every man be swift to hear, slow to speak, slow to wrath" (1:19). This verse emphasizes the importance of active listening and patience in communication. In biblical counseling, counselors should be attentive listeners, allowing the counselees to express themselves fully before offering guidance.

Ineffective communication in biblical counseling keeps the counselor and counselee from understanding each other and can lead to misunderstandings, frustration, and a failure to address the counselee's concerns adequately. The main problems that make communication ineffective are failing to listen actively to the counselee's feelings and perspectives, leading to misunderstandings and a lack of sympathy; using jargon or complex terminology that the counselee does not understand, which can create confusion and hinder effective communication; and not clarifying expectations regarding counseling goals or outcomes, often resulting in misaligned communication and unmet needs.

Both biblical counseling and secular psychology stress the importance of effective communication in counseling. The following are five practices a biblical counselor can implement to promote effective communication in their counseling:

- **Listen Actively:** Engage in active listening, showing compassion for and understanding of the counselee's experiences and emotions.

- **Use Clear and Simple Language:** Avoid jargon or complex language in order to communicate in a direct and straightforward manner.

- **Validate Feelings:** Acknowledge and affirm the counselee's emotions and concerns, creating a safe space for open expression.

- **Clarify Goals and Expectations:** Explain your objectives and expectations to the counselee to ensure mutual understanding and collaboration.

- **Speak Truth in Love:** Offer guidance and feedback in a compassionate and loving manner, promoting a supportive and nurturing counseling environment.

By incorporating effective communication practices into their counseling, biblical counselors can foster a strong therapeutic alliance, promote understanding, and facilitate counselees' growth and healing in alignment with God's truth and grace. Since poor communication skills can lead to misunderstandings, frustration, and a lack of progress in the counseling relationship, every biblical counselor should strive for clarity and active listening.

Emotional Overinvolvement

In the realm of counseling, emotional overinvolvement refers to a situation in which the counselor becomes excessively attached or emotionally invested in the counselee's struggles to the point of compromising professional boundaries. The Bible teaches about healthy relationships, appropriate compassion, and the importance of relying on God for strength. For example, Proverbs 4:23 says, "Keep thy heart with all diligence; for out of it are the issues of life." This verse emphasizes the need to guard one's heart and emotions. In biblical counseling, counselors should maintain appropriate emotional boundaries to prevent overinvolvement. Relying on God's peace can help counselors to manage their emotions in this regard. "The peace of God, which passeth all understanding, shall keep your hearts and minds through Christ Jesus" (Phil 4:6). Paul's instruction to "bear ye one another's burdens, and so fulfil the law of Christ" (Gal 6:2) expresses our calling to support others and help carry their burdens, but there should be a balance between feeling compassion and maintaining professional objectivity. If not, the result may be impaired judgment, boundary violations, and potential harm to both parties.

Emotional overinvolvement occurs when a counselor becomes overly emotionally invested in the counselee's struggles. It can happen in a progression like this. The counselor takes the counselee's problems too personally, leading to heightened emotional reactions. Next comes the blurring of boundaries between the counselor's personal life and professional role. Then the counselor begins to feel compelled to rescue or fix the counselee's problems, potentially undermining the counselee's autonomy and growth.

Both biblical and secular perspectives underscore the importance of maintaining appropriate emotional boundaries in counseling relationships. To address emotional overinvolvement in biblical counseling, counselors should adopt the following practices: (1) ask for God's guidance and rely on His strength to maintain appropriate emotional boundaries; (2) show compassion wisely and sympathize with the counselee while maintaining professional objectivity; (3) be aware of personal triggers or emotional responses that may influence the counseling process and address them prayerfully; (4) seek professional supervision or consultation to discuss challenging cases and to have accountability in maintaining appropriate boundaries; and (5) reinforce counselees' autonomy and encourage them to take responsibility for their own growth and decisions.

By integrating biblical principles of compassion and professional boundaries, biblical counselors can offer compassionate support to their counselees while preserving the integrity of the counseling relationship and ensuring effective and ethical counseling practices. Allowing personal emotions or biases to affect the counseling process can hinder objectivity and compromise the counselee's best interests. Counselors should maintain appropriate professional boundaries.

Unrealistic Expectations

Both counselors and counselees sometimes have expectations that are beyond what can reasonably be achieved through the counseling process. The Bible encourages wisdom, patience, and reliance on God's timing and guidance in all circumstances. "Trust in the Lord with all thine heart; and lean not unto thine own understanding. In all thy ways acknowledge him, and he shall direct thy paths" (Prov 3:5–6). Scripture reminds us to trust in God's guidance and not rely solely on our human understanding. In biblical counseling, counselors and counselees alike should trust in God's plan and timing for growth and healing. The Bible further encourages believers to bring their concerns and desires to God in prayer and supplication. "Be careful for nothing; but in every thing by prayer and supplication with thanksgiving let your requests be made known unto God" (Phil 4:6). In biblical counseling, unrealistic expectations can be addressed through prayer and seeking God's will. It is important to have patience and understand that there is a proper time for everything. In biblical counseling, progress and growth take time, and unrealistic expectations should be managed accordingly. "To every thing there is a season, and a time to every purpose under the heaven" (Eccles 3:1).

It is a common mistake for counselees to look for quick and miraculous solutions to complex problems or to expect the counselor to provide answers beyond the scope of counseling. These expectations may be influenced by societal pressures, misunderstandings about counseling, or previous experiences, and they often take one of three forms:

a. Demanding perfection: Envisioning that counseling will completely resolve all problems and lead to a perfect life without any challenges

b. Hoping for immediate results: Anticipating significant changes and progress after just a few counseling sessions, disregarding the natural progression of personal growth

c. Depending on the counselor: Assuming that the counselor will solve all the issues, ignoring the need for personal effort and responsibility

To preclude problems arising from unrealistic expectations, both counselors and counselees need to be proactive:

- **Set Appropriate Goals:** Establish achievable goals in counseling that align with the counselee's needs and the counseling process.

- **Encourage Patience:** Squelch a quick-fix mentality; instead trust in God's timing for healing and growth.

- **Manage Boundaries:** Counselors should clarify the limits of counseling and help counselees recognize their own role in the counseling journey.

- **Focus on the Process:** Acknowledge that counseling is a process that may require more time and effort than originally thought.

- **Emphasize God's Sovereignty:** Remind counselees that God is in control and that even though His plans may differ from their expectations, He is working out their ultimate good.

Biblical counseling is a gradual process, and growth takes time. Expecting immediate or perfect change can lead to disappointment and discouragement. By operating under realistic expectations, biblical counselors can facilitate a more productive and balanced counseling experience, in which both counselors and counselees work together to seek God's wisdom, guidance, and transformative power in their lives.

Neglecting Self-Care

When counselors fail to take care of their own physical, emotional, and spiritual well-being while serving others, this is the mistake of neglecting self-care. The Bible emphasizes the importance of self-care, recognizing that individuals need strength and renewal to effectively minister to others: "What? know ye not that your body is the temple of the Holy Ghost which is in you, which ye have of God, and ye are not your own? For ye are bought with a price: therefore glorify God in your body, and in your spirit, which are God's" (1 Cor 6:19–20). Here the apostle Paul highlights the significance of taking care of one's body and spirit, recognizing that we belong to God. In biblical counseling, counselors are encouraged to prioritize self-care to honor God with their whole being. Jesus invites those who are weary to find rest in Him. Biblical counselors can find strength and renewal through their relationship with Christ and by practicing self-care. "Come unto me, all ye that labour and are heavy laden, and I will give you rest. Take my yoke upon you, and learn of me; for I am meek and lowly in heart: and ye shall find rest unto your souls. For my yoke is easy, and my burden is light" (Matt 11:28–30).

One of the best-known psalms begins, "The LORD is my shepherd; I shall not want. He maketh me to lie down in green pastures: he leadeth me beside the still waters. He restoreth my soul: he leadeth me in the paths of righteousness for his name's sake" (Ps 23:1–3). The Lord provides rest and restoration for our souls. In biblical counseling, counselors can seek His guidance and care for their own well-being as they help others on their healing journey.

In a secular context, neglecting self-care refers to the counselors' failure to prioritize their own physical, emotional, and mental needs while focusing on supporting others. This neglect can lead to burnout, compassion fatigue, and diminished effectiveness in counseling. These problems can arise in biblical counseling as well. Here are some ways it can happen: overextending (counselors taking on too many counseling sessions or responsibilities, leaving little time for personal rejuvenation), emotional exhaustion (constantly absorbing and carrying the emotional burdens of counselees without processing or addressing their own emotions), and neglecting personal hobbies, relationships, and activities that bring joy and balance to life.

Both biblical and secular perspectives recognize the importance of self-care for counselors. Failing to prioritize self-care can result in counselor burnout and reduced effectiveness. It is essential for counselors to maintain their emotional, physical, and spiritual well-being. All biblical counselors should take the following steps to avoid problems in this area:

- **Prioritize Time with God:** Counselors must spend time in prayer, meditation, and studying God's Word to find strength and guidance for their own lives.

- **Set Personal Boundaries:** Establish healthy limits in counseling relationships to avoid overextending and to ensure adequate time for personal rest and rejuvenation.

- **Seek Support:** Counselors can seek professional supervision, peer support, and accountability to process their emotions and challenges.

- **Engage in Restorative Activities:** Make time for hobbies, exercise, and relationships that bring joy and refreshment.

- **Practice Self-Reflection:** Regularly evaluate personal well-being and assess whether self-care practices are being prioritized.

By implementing self-care practices, biblical counselors can sustain their own well-being and better serve counselees with renewed strength, compassion, and effectiveness, following the biblical principle of loving others as oneself (Mark 12:31).

> **Do you understand everything you have read in this chapter?**
> If not, please read it again before moving on to Chapter 5.

CHAPTER 5

Counseling Techniques and Skills: Practical Methods and Approaches

In biblical counseling, we wholeheartedly embrace the grace of God and extend it to others, recognizing that His love holds the power to bring true healing and restoration.

In the pursuit of effective biblical counseling, this chapter delves into counseling techniques and skills that are valuable tools for guiding individuals toward healing and spiritual growth. As proficient biblical counselors, we understand the paramount importance of placing our complete trust in the Lord while conducting counseling sessions. By embracing our distinctive personalities, appearances, and training as the guidance of the Holy Spirit, we allow God's purposeful design to manifest itself through us as we minister to those in need.

One common error we seek to avoid is giving in to the temptation to alter our identity to fit the counseling role. Since God has uniquely equipped each of us for this divine purpose, we remain steadfast in recognizing that our authenticity lies in God's intentional creation, as affirmed in Psalm 139:14, which says that we are "fearfully and wonderfully made." Using the following practical methods and approaches, we strive to create an environment where the transformative power of God's grace can flow freely, leading counselees on a journey of healing and rediscovering their true selves in Christ. This chapter examines the counseling techniques and skills of listening actively, showing compassion, reflecting, asking open-ended questions, offering encouragement, depending on God in prayer, integrating Scripture, and creating a safe environment.

These practical counseling techniques and skills foster a supportive and compassionate environment for individuals seeking guidance, healing, and personal growth in their lives. By incorporating these approaches into counseling sessions, counselors can help empower counselees to navigate their challenges and discover greater emotional and spiritual well-being.

Active Listening

What it involves
Active listening involves paying full attention to the counselee's verbal and nonverbal cues, demonstrating genuine interest and understanding in what the counselee is sharing, using verbal and nonverbal cues to

indicate attentiveness, such as nodding, maintaining eye contact, and refraining from interrupting or imposing personal judgments during the conversation.

Scriptural basis
As a fundamental and indispensable aspect of biblical counseling, active listening is rooted in the teachings of the Bible, which emphasize the importance of attentive and compassionate listening, both in our relationship with God and with one another.

One of the key passages that highlights the significance of active listening is James 1:19, which says, "Let every man be swift to hear, slow to speak, slow to wrath." This verse instructs us to be quick to listen but not quick to speak or become angry. In the context of counseling, there is great value in patiently and sympathetically listening to the counselee's concerns, struggles, and experiences.

Proverbs 18:13 also emphasizes the importance of active listening: "He that answereth a matter before he heareth it, it is folly and shame unto him." This verse cautions against hasty responses without fully understanding the issue at hand. It encourages biblical counselors to take the time to listen carefully before offering counsel, ensuring that their guidance is founded on a comprehensive understanding of the counselee's situation.

Another proverb reveals the compassionate nature of active listening: "Whoso stoppeth his ears at the cry of the poor, he also shall cry himself, but shall not be heard" (Prov 21:13). If we close our ears to the cries of those in need, we may find ourselves without anyone to hear us when we are in distress. In counseling, active listening demonstrates genuine care and kindness for the counselees' struggles, creating a safe space for them to express their emotions and concerns openly.

Benefits
In biblical counseling, active listening goes beyond hearing words; it also involves paying attention to nonverbal cues and seeking to

understand the underlying emotions and needs of the counselee. By actively engaging in the process of listening, counselors can demonstrate God's love and compassion, providing a supportive environment where healing and growth can occur. Through active listening, counselors can discern the counselees' unique challenges and guide them toward biblical solutions, ultimately fostering spiritual transformation and bringing glory to God in the counseling journey.

Showing Compassion

What it involves
Compassion means showing concern and understanding regarding the counselee's emotions and experiences. The counselor accepts the counselee's feelings and perspectives (rather than minimizing or dismissing them) by using sympathetic statements to convey understanding and support, such as "I can see how that must have been really difficult for you."

Scriptural basis
Compassion is a crucial aspect of biblical counseling and is deeply rooted in the teachings of the Bible. It involves understanding and sharing in the emotions and experiences of others, reflecting the merciful and loving nature of God.

One of the foundational principles of compassion in biblical counseling is found in Romans 12:15: "Rejoice with them that do rejoice, and weep with them that weep." This requires having a genuine connection with others, resonating with their joys and sorrows. In counseling, it means celebrating the counselees' victories and successes while also offering comfort and support during their times of pain and grief.

Similarly, the apostle Peter exhorts believers: "Be ye all of one mind, having compassion one of another, love as brethren, be pitiful, be courteous" (1 Pet 3:8). This emphasizes the importance of showing kindness and understanding toward one another. In biblical counseling, compassion enables counselors to step into the shoes of the counselee, acknowledging their feelings and struggles without being judgmental.

Christ Himself serves as the ultimate example of compassion. "We have not a high priest which cannot be touched with the feeling of our infirmities; but was in all points tempted like as we are, yet without sin" (Heb 4:15). As our High Priest, Jesus understands our weaknesses and temptations, having experienced human emotions and struggles during His time on earth. His example underscores the necessity of sympathizing with others' challenges and being moved by their pain.

Benefits
Biblical counselors are called to exemplify Christ's compassion in their counseling approach. Only in that way can counselors create a safe and caring space for counselees to share their burdens and emotions. Compassion helps counselors understand the deeper motivations and emotions behind the counselee's struggles, leading to more meaningful and effective guidance.

Through active listening and understanding, biblical counselors can address the counselees' needs with compassion and wisdom, pointing them to biblical solutions and ultimately fostering spiritual growth and healing. Compassion reflects the heart of God, who loves and cares for each individual with boundless mercy, offering hope, comfort, and transformation through His Word and the work of the Holy Spirit.

Reflecting

What it involves
The main elements of the reflecting technique include paraphrasing counselees' words to confirm your understanding and to clarify their thoughts by repeating or summarizing the key points the counselee has shared to ensure accurate comprehension, and accurately describing the emotions counselees have expressed to help them process and explore their feelings.

Scriptural basis
Reflecting is a valuable skill in biblical counseling, deeply rooted in the principles of the Bible: "The heart of the righteous studieth to answer: but the mouth of the wicked poureth out evil things" (Prov 15:28). Reflecting allows counselors to carefully consider their responses, taking time to understand the counselee's perspective before offering guidance. It shows respect for the counselee's thoughts and feelings, fostering a deeper connection and trust through the counseling relationship.

Proverbs 25:11 further emphasizes the value of reflecting: "A word fitly spoken is like apples of gold in pictures of silver." When a counselor reflects counselees' emotions and experiences back to them, it provides a thoughtful and meaningful response that brings comfort and encouragement. Reflecting allows counselees to feel heard and understood, validating their feelings and concerns.

By reflecting, counselors also demonstrate the principles of active listening described in James 1:19: "Let every man be swift to hear, slow to speak, slow to wrath" Reflecting allows counselors to be swift to hear the counselee's words, intentionally processing what is being shared before formulating responses. This deliberate approach fosters a harmonious and respectful counseling environment.

Reflecting also aligns with the biblical concept of humility and love for others. "Let nothing be done through strife or vainglory, but in lowliness of mind let each esteem other better than themselves. Look not every man on his own things, but every man also on the things of others" (Phil 2:3–4). By reflecting, counselors demonstrate a humble and caring attitude, prioritizing the counselee's needs and concerns above their own.

Benefits
The use of this technique in biblical counseling serves as a bridge for communication, helping counselors clarify any misunderstandings

and ensuring that they accurately grasp the counselees' emotions and thoughts. By using this skill, counselors can affirm counselees' experiences and guide them to biblical truths that bring healing and transformation.

Ultimately, reflecting helps create a nurturing and supportive counseling atmosphere, allowing the Holy Spirit to work through the counselor to bring clarity, encouragement, and hope to the counselee's journey of healing and growth. In biblical counseling, reflecting exhibits God's desire for genuine and compassionate communication, leading to transformative experiences in the lives of those seeking counsel.

Asking Open-Ended Questions

What it involves

Open-ended questions elicit more than just a simple yes or no. Questions of this type motivate counselees to share more about their experiences and feelings, allowing them to elaborate on their thoughts and perspectives without leading them to specific answers. Examples of open-ended questions include "Tell me more about how that made you feel?" and "What do you think might be contributing to these challenges?"

Scriptural basis

Open-ended questions are a powerful and effective tool in biblical counseling, drawing inspiration from the principles of the Bible. Such questions encourage counselees to express themselves freely, leading to deeper insights and self-discovery.

Proverbs 20:5 emphasizes the value of open-ended questions: "Counsel in the heart of man is like deep water; but a man of understanding will draw it out." In biblical counseling, counselors seek to be understanding and insightful, gently drawing out the counselee's thoughts and emotions through open-ended questions. This allows the counselor to gain a comprehensive understanding of the counselee's heart, needs, and struggles.

Proverbs 25:2 further underscores the importance of open-ended questions: "It is the glory of God to conceal a thing: but the honor of kings is to search out a matter." Open-ended questions enable counselors to explore deeper matters that may not be immediately apparent. This pursuit of understanding honors the counselee" experiences and emotions, and it reflects God's desire for His children to seek wisdom and understanding.

Open-ended questions also align with the biblical principle of loving others: "Thou shalt love thy neighbor as thyself" (Mark 12:31). By using open-ended questions, counselors demonstrate genuine care and interest in the counselee's well-being, fostering a supportive and sympathetic counseling relationship.

Benefits
By using open-ended questions, biblical counselors create a safe space for the counselee to share without fear of judgment or limitation. These questions allow the counselee to express themselves in their own words and at their own pace, encouraging self-reflection and personal growth. In addition, open-ended questions can facilitate spiritual exploration and introspection. They encourage the counselees to consider their faith and relationship with God. This process of self-discovery can lead to profound spiritual insights and growth, aligning with the biblical call to seek God with all our hearts (Jer 29:13).

Overall, this type of question plays a pivotal role in biblical counseling, allowing counselors to understand counselees' unique perspectives, emotions, and needs. Through thoughtful and compassionate use of open-ended questions, biblical counselors create an environment that promotes self-awareness, spiritual exploration, and transformative growth in the counselee's journey toward healing and wholeness in Christ.

Offering Encouragement

What it involves
Offering encouragement involves speaking words of affirmation to mo-

tivate counselees in their journey of growth and healing. The counselor can also acknowledge the counselees' progress and strengths to boost their self-esteem and confidence, providing hope and assurance that positive change is possible with God's help and support.

Scriptural basis
Encouragement is a central pillar of biblical counseling, drawing inspiration from the teachings of the Bible and uplifting and inspiring others through words and actions, fostering hope, and reinforcing their faith in God.

The essence of encouragement is encapsulated in this exhortation: "Wherefore comfort yourselves together, and edify one another, even as also ye do" (1 Thess 5:11). As biblical counselors, we are called to comfort and edify those we counsel, supporting them in their struggles and challenges.

Hebrews 3:13 emphasizes the significance of mutual encouragement: "Exhort one another daily, while it is called To day; lest any of you be hardened through the deceitfulness of sin." This daily mutual encouragement helps combat the deceptions of temptation and strengthens the counselees' resolve to stay faithful to God's Word.

Encouragement is also aligned with the biblical concept of love, the kind of love that "beareth all things, believeth all things, hopeth all things, endureth all things" (1 Cor 13:7). Encouragement demonstrates love by bearing others' burdens, believing in their potential for growth, and instilling hope in their hearts.

In biblical counseling, encouragement plays a vital role in restoring hope and pointing counselees to God's promises. "Whatsoever things were written aforetime were written for our learning, that we through patience and comfort of the scriptures might have hope" (Rom 15:14). As biblical counselors, we use the Scriptures to provide comfort and hope, showing counselees that God's Word is a source of strength and assurance.

Biblically, encouragement is not limited to words alone. As the apostle Paul said, "I have shewed you all things, how that so labouring ye ought to support the weak, and to remember the words of the Lord Jesus, how he said, It is more blessed to give than to receive" (Acts 20:35). Encouragement also involves supporting the weak and showing compassion through acts of kindness and care.

Benefits

In biblical counseling, encouragement fosters a trusting and supportive environment, allowing counselees to experience God's love through the counselor's words and actions. Through encouragement, counselors uplift and motivate counselees, affirming their worth in Christ and guiding them towards positive change.

Encouragement is a powerful catalyst for spiritual growth, as it reminds counselees of God's faithfulness and strengthens their resolve to persevere in their faith. By incorporating encouragement into biblical counseling, counselors demonstrate Christlike love, empowering counselees to face life's challenges with renewed hope and unwavering trust in God's providence.

Dependence on God

What it involves

For biblical counselors, depending on God means seeking His guidance and wisdom through prayer before, during, and after counseling sessions. Another aspect of it is encouraging counselees to bring their concerns and struggles to God in prayer, inviting His intervention, trusting in His sovereignty, and acknowledging Him as the ultimate source of healing and transformation.

Scriptural basis

Prayerful dependence on God is a foundational principle in biblical counseling, deeply rooted in the teachings of the Bible. It involves acknowledging God as the ultimate source of wisdom, guidance, and transformation in the counseling process.

A familiar passage that articulates the core of this concept says, "Trust in the LORD with all thine heart; and lean not unto thine own understanding. In all thy ways acknowledge him, and he shall direct thy paths" (Prov 3:5–6). As biblical counselors, we recognize that our understanding is limited, and we must rely on the Lord completely. Through prayer, we seek His direction and guidance in counseling sessions, trusting that He will lead us on the right path.

Jesus Himself set an example of prayerful dependence on God during His earthly ministry: "In the morning, rising up a great while before day, he went out, and departed into a solitary place, and there prayed" (Mark 1:35). Jesus sought moments of solitude to commune with His Father. In the same way, biblical counselors understand the importance of seeking God's presence through prayer before and during counseling sessions.

Prayerful dependence on God also aligns with the biblical concept of humility: "Humble yourselves in the sight of the Lord, and he shall lift you up" (James 4:10). In counseling, this humility is exemplified through acknowledging our need for divine wisdom and insight because it is only through God's grace and guidance that counselors can offer effective support and direction to counselees.

Paul also emphasizes the role of prayer in finding peace and comfort: "Be careful for nothing; but in every thing by prayer and supplication with thanksgiving let your requests be made known unto God. And the peace of God, which passeth all understanding, shall keep your hearts and minds through Christ Jesus" (Phil 4:6–7). Biblical counselors encourage counselees to bring their concerns and struggles to God in prayer. By doing so, the counselees can experience the peace that surpasses all understanding, trusting that God is in control.

Prayerful dependence on God mainly involves seeking His wisdom through His Word, the Bible. "Thy word is a lamp unto my feet, and a light unto my path" (Ps 119:105). Biblical counselors rely on the Scriptures as the ultimate guide for counseling, knowing that God's Word provides timeless truths and principles for healing and transformation.

Benefits
In biblical counseling, prayerful dependence on God is an ongoing and essential practice. It acknowledges God as the ultimate Counselor and source of wisdom, recognizing that true healing and transformation come through His power and grace. As biblical counselors, we lead counselees to seek God in prayer, encouraging them to rely on His strength and guidance throughout their counseling journey. Through prayerful dependence on God, biblical counselors create an atmosphere where God's transformative work can take place, bringing glory to Him through the lives of those seeking counsel.

Sufficiency in Scripture Alone

What it involves
Understanding that Scripture applied practically to every situation utilizing relevant Bible verses and biblical principles to provide wisdom and guidance in counseling. In this approach the counselor encourages counselees to explore and apply God's Word to their entire lives, specific situations and challenges, as they arise. The biblical counselor will also demonstrate how biblical truths are applied to people's lives for spiritual growth and positive change.

Scriptural basis
Scripture is the fundamental aspect of biblical counseling, based on the truth that the Bible is the ultimate authority and guide for all matters of life, including the issues that cause people to seek counseling.

The fundamental principle is actually the claim the Bible makes about itself: "All scripture is given by inspiration of God, and is profitable for doctrine, for reproof, for correction, for instruction in righteousness: That the man of God may be perfect, thoroughly furnished unto all good works" (2 Tim 3:16–17). Biblical counselors recognize the transformative power of God's Word, which provides essential guidance for teaching, correcting, and leading individuals to righteousness.

In every counseling session, the biblical counselor seeks to introduce scriptural truths and principles to address the counselee's challenges and struggles. The psalmist declares, "Thy testimonies also are my delight and my counselors" (Ps 119:24). As counselors, we draw on the testimonies and teachings of the Bible to offer counsel that aligns with God's will and purposes.

Introducing scripture includes helping counselees apply biblical principles to their lives: "Be ye doers of the word, and not hearers only, deceiving your own selves" (James 1:22). Biblical counselors encourage counselees not only to hear God's Word but also to actively put it into practice in their daily lives. By integrating Scripture into counseling, counselors enable counselees to make godly decisions and experience genuine transformation.

Hebrews 4:12 further highlights the efficacy of God's Word: "The word of God is quick, and powerful, and sharper than any twoedged sword, piercing even to the dividing asunder of soul and spirit, and of the joints and marrow, and is a discerner of the thoughts and intents of the heart." In counseling, Scripture acts as a discerning and illuminating tool, helping counselors understand the counselee's innermost thoughts and motivations.

Benefits
Biblical counselors know that Scripture provides hope and comfort, as affirmed in Romans 15:4, "Whatsoever things were written aforetime were written for our learning, that we through patience and comfort of the scriptures might have hope." By integrating Scriptural truths, counselors offer hope and encouragement to counselees, assuring them of God's unfailing love and grace.

In conclusion, scripture is the core of biblical counseling, ensuring that God's Word serves as the foundation for all counseling principles and methods. By relying on Scripture, biblical counselors provide counsel that is divinely inspired, transformative, and aligned with God's perfect will for the lives of those seeking counsel. Through this approach, biblical counselors offer hope, healing, and guidance to counselees, glorifying God in the counseling journey.

Providing a Safe Environment

What it involves

Providing a safe environment is a matter of finding a comfortable private space where the counselees feel free to confidentially share their thoughts and feelings. It includes establishing an atmosphere of trust through genuine care, respect, and confidence. A nonjudgmental attitude on the part of the counselor will ensure that the counselee feels heard and understood without fear of criticism or rejection.

Scriptural basis

Cultivating an atmosphere of safety and trust is a crucial aspect of biblical counseling, reflecting the biblical principles of love, compassion, and care for others: "To do justice and judgment is more acceptable to the LORD than sacrifice" (Prov 21:3). Biblical counselors strive to be just and fair in their interactions with counselees, ensuring a nonjudgmental situation where individuals feel accepted and valued. The Lord is personally near to those who are brokenhearted: "The LORD is nigh unto them that are of a broken heart; and saveth such as be of a contrite spirit" (Ps 34:18). Biblical counselors apply this truth by creating a safe counseling space where people can share their vulnerabilities and struggles without fear of condemnation or rejection.

This practice also aligns with the biblical concept of humility. "Let nothing be done through strife or vainglory; but in lowliness of mind let each esteem other better than themselves. Look not every man on his own things, but every man also on the things of others" (Phil

2:3–4). By esteeming the needs and concerns of the counselee above their own, counselors demonstrate humility and selflessness, fostering a supportive and compassionate counseling atmosphere.

Moreover, we are encouraged to help our fellow believers: "Bear ye one another's burdens, and so fulfil the law of Christ" (Gal 6:2). In biblical counseling, creating a safe environment involves shouldering counselees' burdens with sympathy and compassion, offering support and encouragement throughout their journey.

James teaches the importance of being slow to give advice and slow to get angry: "Let every man be swift to hear, slow to speak, slow to wrath: for the wrath of man worketh not the righteousness of God" (James 1:19–20). Biblical counselors exemplify these principles by being attentive listeners, showing restraint in their responses, and allowing the counselee's emotions to be expressed without interruption or judgment.

Creating a safe counseling environment also upholds confidentiality. Proverbs emphasizes the value of keeping confidence: "A talebearer revealeth secrets: but he that is of a faithful spirit concealeth the matter" (Prov 11:13). Confidentiality ensures that counselees feel secure in sharing their struggles and concerns, knowing that their private matters will be respected and kept confidential.

Benefits
Overall, cultivating an environment of safety and trust for counseling is essential for establishing a strong relationship. By incorporating the biblical principles of love, humility, and confidentiality, counselors create a nurturing space where counselees can experience God's love, healing, and transformation. This safe environment becomes fertile ground for spiritual growth and positive change in the lives of those seeking counsel, glorifying God throughout the counseling journey.

CHAPTER 6

Master Plan for a Biblical Counseling Session

Jesus's sacrifice on the cross wasn't about boosting our self-esteem; it was about bringing honor to God and saving us from the bondage of sin.

In biblical counseling, every single aspect of the counselor's life—every sin, defeat, victory, relationship, loss, gain, Bible verse pondered and cried over, love, hate, happiness, and even struggles with depression and inadequacies—can be used by our powerful God to display His glory and reveal His merciful love to others. Every counseling session is a unique opportunity for the Lord to work through you to help others in a way that can't be replicated elsewhere in the life of a Christian.

In everything we do, including biblical counseling, let us direct our focus and attention to the omnipotent and holy Savior of the world. As we engage in the counseling process, may His glory and greatness be evident, and may His transformative power work through us to bring healing and restoration to those seeking help. Let our thoughts, words, and actions in the counseling room point to the love, mercy, and wisdom of our Savior, who is the ultimate source of hope and healing for all.

Overview of the Master Plan

- *Review counselee data and prepare counseling agreement.* By understanding the counselees' contexts and circumstances, you can provide more targeted and compassionate guidance in the counseling process.

- *Introduce yourself and establish rapport.* Begin the session with a warm greeting, introducing yourself as the counselor and creating a comfortable and safe atmosphere for the counselee.

- *Start the session with prayer.* Invite the Holy Spirit to guide and lead the counseling process.

- *Listen.* Give the counselee an opportunity to share his or her concerns, struggles, and experiences. Practice active listening as you show concern and understanding.

- *Identify root issues.* Through careful questioning and discernment, seek to uncover the underlying root problems that are contributing to the counselee's challenges.

- *Apply Scripture.* Present relevant biblical principles and truths that address the counselee's specific issues.

- *Reflect and pray.* As you and the counselee consider what has been shared so far, take time to pray together, seeking God's wisdom and direction for the steps to be taken.

- *Set goals.* Collaboratively establish realistic and achievable goals for the counseling process. Ensure that the goals align with biblical principles and the counselee's level of spiritual maturity.

- *Assign homework.* Give instructions for practical exercises or Bible reading to help the counselee apply biblical truths and implement positive life changes.

- *Set up accountability.* Work out a system for regular check-ins and follow-ups to monitor progress and provide ongoing support and encouragement.

- *Address unresolved questions.* Respond to any lingering questions or uncertainties the counselee may have about the counseling process or the biblical principles discussed.

- *Offer encouragement and hope.* Remind the counselee of God's faithfulness and His ability to bring about transformation and healing.

- *Provide resources.* Recommend relevant books, sermons, podcasts, websites, or other resources that can further support the counselee's spiritual growth and understanding.

- *Conclude with prayer.* Summarize the key points discussed during the session, and then pray, committing the counselee's needs to God's care.

- *Document the session.* Take notes on the key issues discussed and the goals set during the session for future reference and continuity in the counseling process.

By following these steps, biblical counseling sessions aim to provide Christ-centered guidance, spiritual support, and practical solutions to help individuals grow in their relationship with God and address the challenges they face.

Detailed Look at Each Step

Data review. Before commencing a counseling session, it is essential to carefully review the data information sheet provided by the counselee and to prepare an agreement to be signed by the counselee.

Bible background. While this specific step is not mentioned in the Bible, several scriptural principles provide guidance on the importance of integrity, accountability, and transparency in the counseling process:

- Proverbs 11:3: "The integrity of the upright shall guide them: but the perverseness of transgressors shall destroy them." Maintaining integrity in counseling involves being truthful, honest, and responsible in handling information provided by the counselee. Reviewing the data information sheet with integrity ensures that the counselor has accurate and relevant information to guide the counseling process effectively.

- Proverbs 15:22: "Without counsel purposes are disappointed: but in the multitude of counsellors they are established." Preparing a counseling agreement allows both the counselor and the counselee to establish clear objectives and expectations for the counseling relationship. This agreement serves as a guiding framework for the counseling process, ensuring that the purposes are established and aligned.

- Colossians 3:9–10: "Lie not one to another, seeing that ye have put off the old man with his deeds; and have put on the new man, which is renewed in knowledge after the image of him that created him." Reviewing the data information sheet and counseling agreement with honesty and transparency reflects the renewal in knowledge and the transformational work of God in the counselor and counselee.

- Proverbs 24:6: "For by wise counsel thou shalt make thy war: and in the multitude of counsellors there is safety." The counseling agreement serves as a form of wise counsel, establishing a safe and supportive environment where both parties understand their roles and responsibilities.

- Matthew 5:37: "Let your communication be, Yea, yea; Nay, nay: for whatsoever is more than these cometh of evil." Preparing a clear and straightforward counseling agreement promotes open and honest communication between the counselor and the counselee, eliminating misunderstandings or misinterpretations.

These principles emphasize the importance of conducting counseling with integrity, accountability, and transparency. By adhering to them, the counselor ensures that the counseling relationship is founded on biblical values, mutual trust, and respect, creating a solid foundation for the counseling journey towards healing, growth, and transformation.

Counselee data sheet. This form typically contains pertinent details of the counselee's personal background, history, current struggles, and specific issues of concern. Pay special attention to names, referrals, local church affiliation (if any), age, marital status, and so on. By reviewing this information, the counselor gains a comprehensive understanding of the counselee's unique situation, which is crucial for providing personalized and effective guidance. During the review process, the counselor may identify patterns, triggers, or underlying root causes of the counselee's challenges. This knowledge enables the counselor to approach the counseling sessions with insight and compassion, demonstrating genuine care and concern for the individual's well-being. Additionally, the data information sheet may highlight any previous counseling experiences, medical conditions, or significant life events that could impact the current counseling process.

Acknowledging and understanding these factors allows the counselor to create a safe and supportive environment, ensuring that the counselee feels heard, valued, and understood.

Counseling agreement. This form typically deals with the following expectations:

1. Confidentiality statement: Clearly define the counselor's commitment to the counselee's privacy, highlighting the limited circumstances in which information may have to be disclosed to outside parties.

2. Goals and objectives: Outline the specific desired outcomes of the counseling process, ensuring that both the counselor and counselee are on the same page.

3. Frequency and duration of sessions: Specify how often and how long counseling sessions will be, ensuring clarity on the time commitment required.

4. Cancellation and rescheduling policy: Set forth the policy for canceling or rescheduling counseling sessions.

5. Fees and payment: If applicable, spell out the financial arrangements.

6. Boundaries and scope: Clarify the limitations of the counseling relationship, specifying the extent of the counselor's role.

7. Informed consent: Be sure that the counselee understands that signing the form acknowledges that he or she understands the agreement and consents to participate in the counseling process.

The counselor should review the counseling agreement with the counselee during the initial counseling session to address any questions or concerns the counselee may have and to ensure full understanding and agreement with the terms outlined in the document. Once both parties are satisfied with the terms, they can sign the form, signifying their commitment to work together collaboratively and confidentially throughout the counseling journey.

In summary, reviewing the data information sheet and preparing the counseling agreement are crucial initial steps in the biblical counseling process. These steps lay the foundation for a trusting and fruitful counseling relationship, ensuring that the counselor and the counselee are aligned in their goals and expectations, ultimately working toward spiritual growth, healing, and transformation.

Introduction

The way you begin the counseling session (i.e., how you introduce yourself and establish rapport) is a critical initial step that involves creating a warm, welcoming, and respectful atmosphere to build trust between the counselor and the counselee. Some biblical principles that inform this process include:

- **Acceptance.** Just as Christ received us with love, grace, and acceptance, biblical counselors should welcome their counselees with the same attitude, treating them with kindness and respect. "Wherefore receive ye one another, as Christ also received us to the glory of God" (Rom 15:7).

- **Openness.** "Counsel in the heart of man is like deep water; but a man of understanding will draw it out" (Prov 20:5). Establishing rapport requires compassion and understanding. A wise and discerning counselor can draw out the counselee's thoughts and feelings, fostering open communication.

- **Caring.** Colossians 3:12 says, "Put on therefore, as the elect of God, holy and beloved, bowels of mercies, kindness, humbleness of mind, meekness, longsuffering." Demonstrating compassion, kindness, humility, and patience reflects the Christlike character that helps build rapport and trust in the counseling relationship.

- **Encouragement.** The counselor should seek to comfort and edify counselees, encouraging them in their journey of growth and healing: "Wherefore comfort yourselves together, and edify one another, even as also ye do" (1 Thess 5:11).

- **Sympathy.** Paul wrote, "To the weak became I as weak, that I might gain the weak: I am made all things to all men, that I might by all means save some" (1 Cor 9:22). Biblical counselors may adapt their approach to connect with counselees on their level, understanding their struggles and vulnerabilities.

- **Forbearance.** The counselor should exercise humility and patience, bearing with the counselee in love, even in challenging situations. As Ephesians 4:2 says: "With all lowliness and meekness, with longsuffering, forbearing one another in love."

- **Solidarity.** The counseling relationship should be characterized by sweet, supportive counsel, walking together in the journey towards God's truth and healing. "We took sweet counsel together, and walked unto the house of God in company" (Ps 55:14).

By incorporating these biblical principles, the counselor demonstrates Christlike love, compassion, and understanding, creating a safe and nurturing environment. In turn, this fosters open communication, allowing the counselees to share their struggles, fears, and hopes more freely. The establishment of rapport paves the way for effective biblical counseling, in which the counselor can offer guidance, support, and biblical solutions tailored to the unique needs of the counselee.

Seeking God's Guidance

Deeply rooted in the teachings of the Bible, the practice of prayer should be an integral aspect of the counseling process because it allows the biblical counselor and the counselees to ask for God's wisdom, direction, and intervention in their journey of healing and growth. Here are some biblical principles that emphasize the significance of prayer in counseling:

Chapter 6

Through prayer, the counselor and counselee can present their concerns, anxieties, and requests to God, finding peace and comfort in His presence. "Be careful for nothing; but in every thing by prayer and supplication with thanksgiving let your requests be made known unto God. And the peace of God, which passeth all understanding, shall keep your hearts and minds through Christ Jesus" (Phil 4:6–7). James promises, "If any of you lack wisdom, let him ask of God, that giveth to all men liberally, and upbraideth not; and it shall be given him" (James 1:5). So, both the counselor and the counselee can seek God's wisdom and discernment through prayer, knowing that God generously provides wisdom to those who ask. Jeremiah records a similar divine promise that counselors and counselees can call on the Lord, trusting that He will answer according to His great and mighty plans for their lives: "Call unto me, and I will answer thee, and shew thee great and mighty things, which thou knowest not" (Jer 33:3).

The psalmist prayed, "Cause me to hear thy lovingkindness in the morning; for in thee do I trust: cause me to know the way wherein I should walk; for I lift up my soul unto thee" (Ps 143:8). Prayer opens the door for the counselor and the counselee to hear God's lovingkindness and seek His guidance in making decisions and navigating life's challenges. Ephesians 6:18 says we should be "praying always with all prayer and supplication in the Spirit, and watching thereunto with all perseverance and supplication for all saints." Prayer should be an ongoing part of the counseling process through which we seek God's guidance, not only for the individual but also for the broader community of believers. It's an attitude of the heart in the counseling relationship, acknowledging our dependence on God's wisdom and leading: "Pray without ceasing" (1 Thess 5:17).

In biblical counseling, prayer plays a vital role in seeking God's intervention, wisdom, and guidance. Both the counselor and the counselee come together in humility and faith, recognizing their need for God's involvement in the healing and transformation process. Through prayer, they invite the Holy Spirit to work in their hearts, bringing comfort, peace, and revelation of God's truth. A counselor's reliance on prayer demonstrates trust in God's sovereignty, while the counselees' participation in prayer reveals their openness to God's healing touch and the desire for His will to be manifested in their lives. Together, they embark on a journey of seeking God's guidance, knowing that He is the ultimate Counselor and Healer who leads them on the path of restoration and spiritual growth.

Active Listening

Even though the term active listening is not used in the Bible, the concept is deeply rooted in biblical principles. It involves fully engaging with the speaker, focusing on his or her words, emotions, and underlying messages. Here are eight biblical principles that align with the practice of active listening:

1. James 1:19: "Wherefore, my beloved brethren, let every man be swift to hear, slow to speak, slow to wrath." This verse promotes a humble and patient approach in communication with others.

2. Proverbs 18:13: "He that answereth a matter before he heareth it, it is folly and shame unto him." Active listening entails fully hearing and understanding what the other person is saying before formulating a response. Jumping to conclusions without listening can lead to misunderstandings and embarrassment.

3. Proverbs 15:31: "The ear that heareth the reproof of life abideth among the wise." Active listening involves being receptive to constructive criticism and correction, leading to wisdom and growth.

4. Matthew 11:15: "He that hath ears to hear, let him hear." Jesus often encouraged His followers to have attentive ears, indicating the importance of listening to His teachings and messages.

5. Romans 12:15: "Rejoice with them that do rejoice, and weep with them that weep." Active listening goes beyond hearing words; it

involves empathizing with the speakers' emotions and sharing in their joys and sorrows.

6. Proverbs 12:15: "The way of a fool is right in his own eyes: but he that hearkeneth unto counsel is wise." By actively listening to the counsel of others, we demonstrate wisdom and humility, recognizing that we don't have all the answers.

7. Proverbs 20:5: "Counsel in the heart of man is like deep water; but a man of understanding will draw it out." Active listening requires a discerning and understanding heart to elicit the deeper thoughts and feelings of the speaker.

8. James 1:22: "Be ye doers of the word, and not hearers only, deceiving your own selves." Active listening extends to putting into practice what is heard and understood, living out God's Word in daily life.

While active listening is not explicitly mentioned in Scripture, the underlying principles of attentiveness, humility, compassion, and wise discernment align with biblical teaching. Engaging in active listening in the counseling context demonstrates respect, love, and a desire to truly understand and support others, making it an essential component of effective communication and building strong relationships in the Christian context.

Identification of Root Issues

In biblical counseling, the process of determining root problems is essential for understanding the underlying causes and motives behind the counselees' struggles and challenges. Although the term root issues does not appear anywhere in the Bible, the concept aligns with various biblical principles that emphasize the significance of examining the heart and inner motives.

Scripture highlights the importance of guarding the heart because it is the source of life's outcomes. Identifying root issues involves delving into the heart to understand its condition and motivations. "Keep thy heart with all diligence; for out of it are the issues of life" (Prov 4:23). The Old Testament taught that the heart can be deceptive and filled with hidden motives. "The heart is deceitful above all things, and desperately wicked: who can know it?" (Jer 17:9). Jesus said, "From within, out of the heart of men, proceed evil thoughts, adulteries, fornications, murders, thefts, covetousness, wickedness, deceit, lasciviousness, an evil eye, blasphemy, pride, foolishness: all these evil things come from within, and defile the man" (Mark 7:21–23). Identifying root issues involves recognizing the fallen nature of humanity and the need for God's discernment to uncover hidden sins, and it helps to address the internal conditions that lead to outward behaviors.

Scriptural Application

As the core of the biblical counseling session, this step involves interpreting life's challenges and struggles through the lens of God's Word and applying its principles to find guidance, healing, and transformation. This concept aligns closely with what the Bible says about the importance of seeking God's wisdom and living according to His truth. Scripture is divinely inspired and has the power to guide, correct, and equip believers for righteous living. "All scripture is given by inspiration of God, and is profitable for doctrine, for reproof, for correction, for instruction in righteousness: that the man of God may be perfect, thoroughly furnished unto all good works" (2 Tim 3:16–17).

In biblical counseling, a biblical perspective provides the foundation for offering sound advice and direction. This is clearly taught in the Old Testament: "Thy word is a lamp unto my feet, and a light unto my path" (Ps 119:105). "The law of the LORD is perfect, converting the soul: the testimony of the Lord is sure, making wise the simple. The statutes of the LORD are right, rejoicing the heart: the commandment of the LORD is pure, enlightening the eyes"(Ps 19:7–8). God's Word serves as a guiding light, illuminating the right path to follow in every situation. In biblical counseling, applying a biblical perspective means seeking God's wisdom through His Word to discern the best course of action as we draw on God's statutes and commandments to find true transformation and inner peace.

Turning to the New Testament, we see the same principle: "Be not conformed to this world: but be ye transformed by the renewing of your mind, that ye may prove what is that good, and acceptable, and perfect, will of God" (Rom 12:2). Applying a biblical perspective involves renewing the mind with God's truth, rejecting worldly thinking, and aligning with God's will. In counseling, this transformation leads to finding God's perfect plan for one's life. A biblical perspective shifts the focus from earthly concerns to heavenly matters, prioritizing spiritual growth and obedience to God's Word. As Colossians 3:2 puts it, "Set your affection on things above, not on things on the earth." In biblical counseling, a biblical perspective goes beyond hearing God's Word to applying it actively in daily life. This active obedience brings true transformation. "Be ye doers of the word, and not hearers only, deceiving your own selves" (James 1:22). Jesus declared, "Whosoever heareth these sayings of mine, and doeth them, I will liken him unto a wise man, which built his house upon a rock" (Matt 7:24). Building life on the solid foundation of God's Word, and applying biblical principles, leads to a stable and wise life.

Adopting a biblical perspective means relying on God's Word as the ultimate source of truth and wisdom. It involves interpreting life's challenges, emotions, and experiences through the lens of Scripture. By doing so, the counselor and counselee gain God's perspective and apply His principles to find direction, healing, and purpose. This transformative process leads to a deeper relationship with God, increased spiritual growth, and the ability to face life's trials with confidence and hope in Christ.

Prayerful Reflection

In biblical counseling, prayerful reflection is a vital practice that involves seeking God's wisdom, discernment, and guidance through prayer as counselors and counselees examine their own experiences, emotions, and thoughts. This concept flows out of various passages that emphasize the importance of prayer and self-examination. Here are five examples:

- 1 Thessalonians 5:17: "Pray without ceasing." In counseling, prayerful reflection means maintaining a continuous attitude of prayer, seeking God's presence and wisdom throughout the counseling process.

- Psalm 139:23–24: "Search me, O God, and know my heart: try me, and know my thoughts: and see if there be any wicked way in me, and lead me in the way everlasting." Prayerful reflection involves inviting God to examine our thoughts and motives and lead us in the path of righteousness.

- Psalm 19:14: "Let the words of my mouth, and the meditation of my heart, be acceptable in thy sight, O LORD, my strength, and my redeemer." Prayerful reflection includes offering thoughts and emotions to God, seeking His acceptance, and acknowledging Him as the source of strength and redemption.

- Lamentations 3:40: "Let us search and try our ways, and turn again to the LORD." Prayerful reflection leads to self-examination and repentance, turning to the Lord for forgiveness and guidance.

- Psalm 119:15: "I will meditate in thy precepts, and have respect unto thy ways." Prayerful reflection includes meditating on God's precepts and aligning ourselves with His ways.

In biblical counseling, prayerful reflection is a powerful practice that helps individuals gain insight, find peace, and discern God's will in their lives. It involves seeking God's presence, meditating on His

Word, and being receptive to His leading. During prayerful reflection, counselors and counselees open their hearts before God, seeking His guidance and direction in every aspect of the counseling process. This practice fosters spiritual growth, a deeper connection with God, and a greater understanding of His purpose amid life's challenges. As counselors and counselees engage in prayerful reflection, they open themselves to God's transformative work, allowing Him to shape their thoughts, attitudes, and actions according to His divine plan.

Goal Setting

Setting goals in a biblical counseling context involves seeking God's wisdom and aligning with His Word to establish clear objectives for the counseling process. Although the specific term goal setting is not mentioned in the Bible, numerous passages emphasize the importance of seeking God's guidance and direction in every aspect of life, including counseling.

"Commit thy works unto the Lord, and thy thoughts shall be established (Prov 16:3). In biblical counseling, setting goals requires committing the process to the Lord, seeking His guidance, and trusting that He will establish the right path. In Psalm 32:8, God promises, "I will instruct thee and teach thee in the way which thou shalt go: I will guide thee with mine eye." The apostle Paul's approach to goal setting entailed focusing on the future and leaving behind past failures to pursue God's call. "I count not myself to have apprehended: but this one thing I do, forgetting those things which are behind, and reaching forth unto those things which are before, I press toward the mark for the prize of the high calling of God in Christ Jesus" (Phil 3:13–14). Based on this, we should encourage counselees to align their personal desires with God's counsel, recognizing that His plans will ultimately prevail. "There are many devices in a man's heart; nevertheless, the counsel of the LORD, that shall stand" (Prov 19:21).

Goal setting in biblical counseling refers to collaboratively defining specific achievable objectives that counselees aim to accomplish during the course of their counseling journey. These goals should be derived from a biblical framework, seeking to address the root issues, promote spiritual growth, and align with God's will for the individual's life.

In setting goals, the counselor and the counselee work together to identify areas for improvement and transformation. The counselor listens attentively to the counselees' concerns, struggles, and aspirations, seeking to understand their unique needs and challenges. The goals set during the counseling session are typically measurable, time-bound, and realistic. They might include goals like these:

- Strengthening one's relationship with God through prayer, Bible study, and regular church attendance

- Overcoming specific sinful behaviors or negative thought patterns through accountability and biblical strategies

- Developing healthier coping mechanisms for dealing with stress, anxiety, or depression

- Improving communication and resolving conflicts in relationships, based on biblical principles of love, forgiveness, and reconciliation

- Gaining a deeper understanding of God's love and grace, leading to increased self-esteem and confidence

The counselor ought to provide encouragement, support, and guidance throughout the counseling process, helping the counselee stay focused on the established goals. Periodic reviews and adjustments may be made as needed, considering the progress made and addressing any new challenges that arise.

Ultimately, goal setting in counseling combines the wisdom and guidance of God's Word with practical strategies to facilitate growth, healing, and transformation in the counselee's life, fostering a deeper relationship with God and a more fulfilling life journey.

Homework Assignments

Using homework assignments is consistent with various biblical principles that emphasize the importance of actively applying God's Word to one's life and nurturing spiritual growth. James 1:22 says, "Be ye doers of the word, and not hearers only, deceiving your own selves." Homework assignments can be designed to encourage counselees to apply biblical principles in their daily lives. The psalmist said, "Thy word have I hid in mine heart, that I might not sin against thee" (Ps 119:11). Assigning Scriptures to memorize or meditate on can help counselees internalize biblical truths and resist temptations. Similarly, assignments that encourage counselees to immerse themselves in God's Word and engage in worshipful practices promote spiritual growth and transformation. "Let the word of Christ dwell in you richly in all wisdom; teaching and admonishing one another in psalms and hymns and spiritual songs, singing with grace in your hearts to the Lord" (Col 3:16). Paul warned the first-century believers: "Be not conformed to this world: but be ye transformed by the renewing of your mind, that ye may prove what is that good, and acceptable, and perfect, will of God" (Rom 12:2). Homework can be designed to challenge counselees to renew their minds through the study and application of Scripture, aligning their lives with God's will.

Homework assignments—tasks or activities given to counselees to do between counseling sessions—are intended to reinforce the biblical principles presented, to promote self-reflection, and to ignite personal growth and change.

Examples of homework assignments in biblical counseling might include

1. *Bible study and reflection* to encourage the counselee to read specific passages, meditate on them, and journal their thoughts and insights;

2. *prayer prompts and devotional exercises* to deepen the counselee's prayer life and connection with God;

3. *application of biblical principles* to real-life situations, such as forgiving others, showing love and kindness, or seeking reconciliation;

4. *gratitude journals* to help counselees cultivate a spirit of gratefulness by writing down things they are thankful for each day;

5. *self-care activities* that promote physical, emotional, and spiritual well-being, such as exercise, rest, or spending time in nature; and

6. *accountability* by partnering with someone from the local church community who will give support and encouragement.

Homework assignments serve as a bridge between counseling sessions, allowing the counselee to reflect on insights gained and to practice new skills or attitudes. They provide opportunities for personal exploration, self-awareness, and spiritual development. The counselor may review completed assignments in subsequent sessions, providing feedback, encouragement, and further guidance as needed. By integrating biblical principles into homework assignments, the counselor seeks to motivate counselees to take ownership of their spiritual growth and transformation, fostering a deeper connection with God and a more profound understanding of His Word.

Accountability

As a feature of biblical counseling, accountability is a fundamental practice that involves believers supporting and encouraging one another to live in accordance with God's Word and holding each other responsible for actions and attitudes. The various aspects of this concept are firmly rooted in Scripture.

Burden bearing: "Brethren, if a man be overtaken in a fault, ye which are spiritual, restore such a one in the spirit of meekness; considering thyself, lest thou also be tempted. Bear ye one another's burdens, and so fulfil the law of Christ" (Gal 6:1–2). Biblical counseling emphasizes the importance of accountability within the Christian community. Believers are called to gently restore and support one another in times of struggle, bearing each other's burdens as an expression of Christ's love.

Mutuality: Proverbs 27:17 says, "Iron sharpeneth iron; so a man sharpeneth the countenance of his friend." Accountability in biblical counseling fosters mutual encouragement and growth among fellow believers.

Provocation: Biblical counseling encourages believers to consider each other and use accountability relationships to stir each other up to love people and to do good deeds. "Let us consider one another to provoke unto love and to good works" (Heb 10:24).

Confession: James exhorts believers, "Confess your faults one to another, and pray one for another, that ye may be healed. The effectual fervent prayer of a righteous man availeth much" (James 5:16). Accountability entails the willingness to admit faults and shortcomings to our brothers and sisters and seek prayer support for healing and restoration.

Responsibility: Accountability in biblical counseling counselees take responsibility for their own actions, attitudes, and behaviors within a supportive and caring counseling relationship. It involves the counselor guiding the counselee toward self-awareness, self-reflection, and personal growth.

Accountability methods used in biblical counseling include the following:

1. Encouraging self-reflection: The counselor helps counselees explore their thoughts, emotions, and behaviors, fostering a deeper understanding of their challenges and the underlying root issues.
2. Formulating objectives and action plans: The counselor and counselee work together to set specific and achievable goals, with

the counselor providing support and encouragement as the counselee works toward these goals.

3. Conducting regular check-ins: The counselor schedules follow-up sessions to monitor the counselee's progress, discuss challenges, and celebrate successes.

4. Forming partnerships: The counselor may encourage the counselee to connect with an accountability partner from his or her church or community to receive additional support and encouragement outside the counseling sessions.

5. Evaluating progress: The counselor and counselee should periodically review the progress being made and adjust strategies and approaches as needed.

6. Emphasizing prayer and spiritual growth: In a biblical context, accountability also involves encouraging counselees to engage in prayer, Bible study, and other spiritual practices to strengthen their relationship with God.

Accountability in biblical counseling provides a safe and nonjudgmental space for individuals to examine their lives, grow in self-awareness, and take positive steps toward personal transformation. The counselor serves as a supportive guide, helping counselees navigate challenges and celebrate progress on their journey of healing and growth. The ultimate aim is to help each counselee align his or her life with God's truth in order to experience the fullness of life that comes from walking in obedience to His Word.

Unresolved Questions

Addressing unresolved issues in biblical counseling involves seeking God's wisdom, guidance, and understanding through His Word to find answers and clarity. Various biblical principles come into play here. The biblical counselor should take unresolved questions to God in prayer, asking for wisdom, and trusting in His promise to provide guidance and understanding rather than relying on human wisdom. "If any of you lack wisdom, let him ask of God, that giveth to all men liberally, and upbraideth not; and it shall be given him (James 1:5). "Trust in the Lord with all thine heart; and lean not unto thine own understanding. In all thy ways acknowledge him, and he shall direct thy paths" (Prov 3:5–6). God's Word serves as a source of illumination when addressing unresolved questions, guiding believers in making decisions and finding direction. "Thy word is a lamp unto my feet, and a light unto my path" (Ps 119:105).

Biblical counseling seeks to bring clarity to unresolved questions, recognizing that God is a God of order and peace, not confusion. As 1 Corinthians 14:33 explains, "God is not the author of confusion, but of peace, as in all churches of the saints."

How should a biblical counselor address unresolved questions? Here are some ways:

- **Engage in Active Listening:** The counselor attentively listens to the counselees' concerns and emotions, acknowledging the difficult aspects of their experiences and responding with kindness.

- **Explore Biblical Perspectives:** The counselor helps counselees grasp relevant passages of Scripture that relate to their questions and struggles.

- **Emphasize Prayer for God's Guidance:** Prayer is vital in seeking God's direction and finding answers to unresolved questions.

- **Provide Perspective:** The counselor offers viewpoints and insights that align with biblical principles, guiding counselees toward a deeper understanding of their concerns.

- **Encourage Self-Reflection:** The counselee is encouraged to engage in self-reflection to reevaluate personal beliefs and values in light of biblical truths.

- **Offer Patience and Support:** Addressing unresolved questions may be a process that requires time and endurance. The counselor provides ongoing support and encouragement throughout this journey.

From both the biblical and secular perspectives, addressing unresolved questions in counseling involves seeking understanding and guidance. While the biblical approach prioritizes God's Word and prayer, the secular approach focuses on providing sympathetic support and guiding the counselee toward self-discovery and personal growth. By addressing unresolved questions in a compassionate and thoughtful manner, biblical counseling seeks to bring clarity, peace, and a deeper connection with God's truth and wisdom.

Encouragement and Hope

Encouragement and hope are central themes in biblical counseling, rooted in the promises and teachings of the Bible. Scripture contains a wealth of passages on comfort, guidance, and assurance that serve as a source of encouragement and hope for those seeking counsel. Biblical counseling offers hope by assuring counselees that even in their brokenness, God is near and ready to heal and save those with a humble and repentant heart.

> "The Lord is nigh unto them that are of a broken heart; and saveth such as be of a contrite spirit" (Ps 34:18).

> "They that wait upon the Lord shall renew their strength; they shall mount up with wings as eagles; they shall run, and not be weary, and they shall walk, and not faint" (Is 40:31).

> "Whatsoever things were written aforetime were written for our learning, that we through patience and comfort of the scriptures might have hope" (Rom 15:4).

Chapter 6

"I know the thoughts that I think toward you, saith the Lord, thoughts of peace, and not of evil, to give you an expected end" (Jer 29:11).

The Bible provides comfort and hope through its teachings, offering wisdom and examples from the past that can inspire and encourage counselees in their present challenges and assuring counselees that God has a plan for their lives, filled with hope and a future of peace and purpose.

While the secular perspective does not involve the use of Scripture, it recognizes the significance of fostering hope and optimism within the counseling relationship. In biblical counseling, the counselor's role is to provide support, motivation, and positive reinforcement to the counselee. Here are some ways a biblical counselor can do that:

1. *Affirm and validate:* The counselor affirms the counselee's strengths, efforts, and progress, providing positive reinforcement.

2. *Set realistic goals:* The counselor works with the counselee to establish achievable goals, fostering a sense of hope and motivation for change.

3. *Offer sympathy and understanding:* Encouragement comes through active listening and showing compassion, acknowledging the counselee's experiences and feelings.

4. *Suggest strategies for coping:* The counselor equips counselees with coping skills and problem-solving techniques, empowering them to navigate challenges with confidence.

5. *Highlight resilience:* The counselor may help counselees recognize their own resilience and ability to overcome difficulties, inspiring hope for the future.

Both biblical and secular perspectives regarding the role of encouragement and hope in counseling aim to uplift and support the counselee, fostering a positive outlook and a sense of assurance. By drawing from scriptural teachings or principles, biblical counselors strive to inspire hope, resilience, and a greater sense of purpose and meaning in their counselees. For believers, the ultimate source of encouragement and hope lies in God's promises and the transformative power of His Word.

Resources

In biblical counseling, providing resources involves guiding counselees to the wisdom found in God's Word and other Bible-based materials. Although people who lived in Bible times did not have access to most of the resources available today, the concept of providing resources aligns with the biblical principle of seeking knowledge and understanding from God's Word.

Biblical counseling emphasizes the importance of seeking wisdom and understanding from God, the ultimate source of knowledge. "The LORD giveth wisdom: out of his mouth cometh knowledge and understanding" (Prov 2:6). Since "all scripture is given by inspiration of God, and is profitable for doctrine, for reproof, for correction, for instruction in righteousness" (2 Tim 3:16), providing biblical resources enables counselees to draw from the inspired Word of God, equipping them for righteous living.

Resources based on Scripture serve as a guiding light, providing clarity and direction for counselees' journeys. "Thy word is a lamp unto my feet, and a light unto my path" (Ps 119:105). Finally, Colossians 3:16 says, "Let the word of Christ dwell in you richly in all wisdom; teaching and admonishing one another in psalms and hymns and spiritual songs, singing with grace in your hearts to the Lord." Providing resources that help counselees immerse themselves in the Word fosters spiritual growth and a deeper relationship with Christ.

In biblical counseling, various materials, tools, and references that complement the counseling process can support the counselee's growth and development. These resources may include books, articles, videos, podcasts, workbooks, or other materials that align with biblical principles and provide practical insights. Types of resources include the following:

- *Biblical study guides* or devotionals that delve into specific biblical themes or books to help counselees deepen their understanding of God's Word.

- *Christian books* by reputable Christian authors that address relevant topics and offer spiritual insights

- *Sermons and podcasts* (audio or video) that explore biblical teachings and offer practical applications for daily living

- *Worship songs* that reinforce biblical truths and encourage counselees spiritually

- *Prayer journals* to help counselees record their prayers, thoughts, and reflections

- *Scripture memory cards* to help counselees memorize and meditate on God's Word

Taking advantage of the abundance of resources available today, biblical counselors seek to empower counselees with additional tools and knowledge to grow spiritually, navigate challenges, and deepen their understanding of God's truth. These resources complement the counseling process, enhancing the counselees' engagement and equipping them to apply biblical principles in their daily lives.

Conclusion of the Session

In biblical counseling, the culmination of a counseling session is a s ignificant moment when the counselor and counselee recap the insights gained, discuss progress made, and plan for future steps. It is a time to reiterate the importance of seeking God's guidance, putting faith into action, and relying on His strength for the journey ahead. Prayer plays a central role in wrapping up a biblical counseling session since it brings the concerns, successes, and hopes before God, seeking His continued guidance and support.

This practice aligns with the following Scriptures:

- Philippians 1:6: "Being confident of this very thing, that he which hath begun a good work in you will perform it until the day of Jesus Christ." The conclusion of a counseling session offers hope that God, who began the good work in the counselees, will continue to transform and shape them until the day of Christ's return.

- 2 Corinthians 1:3–4: "Blessed be God, even the Father of our Lord Jesus Christ, the Father of mercies, and the God of all comfort; who comforteth us in all our tribulation, that we may be able to comfort them which are in any trouble, by the comfort wherewith we ourselves are comforted of God." In the concluding portion of a counseling session, the counselor and counselee find comfort in the knowledge that God is the source of all comfort, and this comfort can be shared with others facing similar challenges.

- 1 Thessalonians 5:17: "Pray without ceasing." Prayer is an essential part of the biblical counseling session from start to finish. It is a continuous act of seeking God's presence, wisdom, and guidance in all aspects of life.

- Psalm 138:3: "In the day when I cried thou answeredst me, and strengthenedst me with strength in my soul." Conclude the counseling session by acknowledging God's faithfulness in answering prayers and strengthening the soul during times of distress.

The final minutes of a counseling session should be devoted to the following activities:

1. **Reviewing**—The counselor recaps the key insights and strategies discussed during the session, ensuring clarity and understanding.

2. **Planning**—The counselor and counselee collaboratively set achievable goals for the counselee to work until the next session, promoting personal growth and development.

3. **Encouraging**—The counselor offers words of encouragement and hope based on the progress made and reiterates the counselee's strengths and potential for positive change.

4. **Praying**—Either the counselor or the counselee may pray aloud, asking for God's guidance, strength, and blessing.

5. **Scheduling**—Discuss the timing of the next meeting, assuring the counselee of your availability for questions and providing a sense of continuity and ongoing support.

In secular counseling, the conclusion of a session focuses on practical steps and strategies to work on between sessions, empowering counselees to implement positive changes in their lives. In biblical counseling, however, prayer is the most important element of the end of the session. Acknowledging God's role in the counseling process and seeking His ongoing involvement in the counselee's life, it is an expression of dependence and gratitude, seeking divine wisdom for continued growth and transformation. The conclusion of a biblical counseling session should leave counselees with a sense of hope, clarity, and encouragement as they continue their journey of healing, growth, and self-discovery.

Documentation

In counseling, documentation refers to the practice of recording important details, insights, and progress made during counseling sessions. Though this practice is not mentioned in the Bible, the concept aligns with biblical principles of diligence, accountability, and recording significant events. (1) "A prudent man foreseeth the evil, and hideth himself: but the simple pass on, and are punished" (Prov 22:3). Session documentation reflects prudence, as it allows both the counselor and the counselee to foresee patterns, challenges, and progress, enabling them to make informed decisions and avoid pitfalls. (2) "The thoughts of the diligent tend only to plenteousness, but of every one that is hasty only to want" (Prov 21:5). Diligent documentation helps counselors and counselees focus on fruitful outcomes, ensuring that decisions and strategies are adequately thought out and effective. (3) "To every thing there is a season, and a time to every purpose under the heaven" (Eccles 3:1). Documenting each counseling session acknowledges the different seasons of the counseling journey, helping to track growth, identify recurring issues, and adapt approaches accordingly. (4) "God is not the author of confusion, but of peace, as in all churches of the saints" (1 Cor 14:33). Keeping records promotes clarity and order, ensuring that both the counselor and the counselee can have a clear understanding of the counseling process.

In counseling, the systematic recording of information, discussions, and insights during counseling sessions is a vital aspect of maintaining an organized and efficient counseling practice, providing a reference for future sessions, and ensuring continuity and progress in the counseling process.

Session documentation serves various purposes in biblical counseling, such as providing a reference for the counselor to prepare for future sessions and assess progress, facilitating communication with other counselors or professionals involved in the counselee's care, demonstrating accountability and professionalism in the counseling relationship, ensuring consistency in the counseling process, even if multiple counselors are involved, and allowing counselees to track their own growth and progress throughout the counseling journey.

Such documentation may include the following:

- **Case Notes:** Detailed notes on the counselee's background, concerns, goals, and progress made during each session

- **Counseling Plans:** Records of the strategies, interventions, goals, and action plans discussed and agreed on with the counselee

- **Prayer Requests:** Notes about specific prayer needs shared by the counselee and any answered prayers or significant spiritual insights

- **Progress Tracking:** Documentation of improvements, setbacks, or changes in the counselee's attitudes, behaviors, and emotions

- **Homework Assignments:** List of the homework assigned to counselees and their responses to these assignments

- **Reflections and Insights:** Summary any significant insights gained during a session and potential implications for future sessions

Overall, recordkeeping in counseling is a valuable tool that enhances the effectiveness and continuity of the process, facilitating a more organized and purposeful approach to helping individuals grow and find healing in their lives.

> **Do you understand everything you have read in this chapter?**
> If not, please read it again before moving on to Chapter 7.

CHAPTER 7

Self-Examination and Self-Care for Counselors

In biblical counseling, we learn that our value and worth are not defined by our past mistakes. Instead, we are cherished and loved unconditionally by our Heavenly Father. Our past does not dictate our identity; it is the grace and love of God that shapes who we truly are. Through biblical counseling, we discover the freedom to let go of guilt and shame, embracing our true worth in the eyes of our loving Creator.

As biblical counselors, we wholeheartedly embrace the hurts and struggles of those we counsel. Biblical counseling is an all-encompassing endeavor, offering an opportunity to extend help and support to those who are seeking solace and guidance from their Lord and Savior through this approach. To be a counselor is a divine calling, as the Lord has chosen us to be instruments of His healing and restoration in their lives.

However, we must be careful not to form a deep, almost familial bond with our counselees because that can lead to feeling an undue sense of responsibility for their successes and failures. We must remember that the victories ultimately belong to the Lord, and the struggles are inherent to our fellow imperfect beings, whom we have the privilege to assist.

To ensure that we do not become unnecessarily burdened, we must continuously seek the Lord's will and direction through self-examination and self-care. By looking inward and evaluating our own motivations, emotions, and well-being, we can maintain a healthy perspective and better serve those in need. Our commitment to self-care allows us to replenish and strengthen ourselves, making us more effective vessels of God's love and guidance in the counseling process.

Under the Lord's guidance, self-examination and self-care are vital aspects of biblical counseling, aligning with the theme of seeking spiritual growth and effectiveness in the counseling process.

The apostle Paul encourages believers to examine themselves: "Examine yourselves, whether ye be in the faith; prove your own selves" (2 Cor 13:5). In biblical counseling, counselors must regularly engage in self-examination to ensure they are rooted in their faith and relying on Christ. By examining their own hearts and motives, counselors can better serve counselees in humility and God-centeredness.

Self-care is also emphasized in the Bible. Jesus advised His disciples to rest: "Come ye yourselves apart into a desert place, and rest a while: for there were many coming and going, and they had no leisure so much as to eat" (Mark 6:31). Similarly, biblical counselors are called to take moments of rest and renewal, recognizing that caring for themselves enables them to better care for others.

Self-examination and self-care also align with the biblical concept of love for oneself. Jesus commands us, "Love thy neighbor as thyself" (Matt 22:39). This verse implies that we should love ourselves in a healthy and balanced way, understanding that we are valuable creations of God. Self-care is an expression of self-love, ensuring that counselors prioritize their physical, emotional, and spiritual well-being.

The Bible also reminds us that our bodies are temples of the Holy Spirit: "Know ye not that your body is the temple of the Holy Ghost which is in you, which ye have of God, and ye are not your own? For ye are bought with a price: therefore glorify God in your body, and in your spirit, which are God's" (1 Cor 6:19–20). As biblical counselors, taking care of our bodies and physical well-being is a way to honor God and His dwelling within us.

Furthermore, self-examination helps counselors identify their limitations and seek appropriate support when needed. "In the multitude of counselors there is safety" (Prov 11:14). Seeking guidance from mentors, peers, or supervisors allows counselors to gain insight, grow in their skills, and ensure ethical and effective counseling practices.

Self-care also involves setting healthy boundaries to prevent burnout and compassion fatigue. "Let us not be weary in well doing: for in due season we shall reap, if we faint not" (Gal 6:9). By prioritizing self-care, counselors can sustain their effectiveness and continue to sow seeds of hope and healing in the lives of counselees.

In conclusion, self-examination and self-care are crucial for biblical counselors. By engaging in regular self-examination, counselors maintain a humble and God-centered approach to counseling. Prioritizing self-care enables counselors to be refreshed and equipped to support others effectively. Embracing self-examination and self-care, counselors exemplify God's love and grace to those they serve, fostering a fruitful and transformative counseling experience.

CHAPTER 8

Mandatory Reporting

Helping one person might not change the whole world, but it will change the world for one person.

Mandatory Reporting

Throughout this book, I have emphasized the importance of mandatory reporting. Over the course of countless hours, I have listened to the stories of those deeply wounded by the evils of this world, and it is disheartening to realize that some of them did not receive the help they deserved from those who should have been there to support them. A single report could have made a world of difference for many of these individuals. When I complied with the law and reported each case, the result was the discovery of others who had suffered at the hands of the same abusers and in some instances the arrest of the perpetrator.

Mandatory reporting, also known as mandated reporting, is the legal obligation of certain individuals to report known or suspected cases of abuse, neglect, or harm to the designated authorities. Its purpose is to protect vulnerable individuals, including children, the elderly, and those with disabilities, from potential harm or dangerous situations.

God's Word unequivocally emphasizes your responsibility as a counselor to care for His people. As a mandated reporter, if you disregard the Lord's direction and fail in your duty, you are not fit to serve as a counselor or in any other service called by the Lord. Be aware you are not called to investigate as a police officer or an investigator, but you are a safe harbor, representing an omnipotent God. If you are informed about any harmful situation, it is your solemn duty to report it immediately, ensuring the safety and well-being of those at risk. Do not shirk your duty.

Mandatory reporting requirements vary from one jurisdiction to another since they are determined by the laws and regulations of each country, state, or region. Generally, mandatory reporting applies to professionals and individuals who have regular contact with vulnerable populations. These may include teachers, healthcare professionals, clergy, social workers, counselors, law enforcement officers, or anyone who can provide assistance to someone in need or distress.

When persons subject to mandatory reporting become aware of any form of abuse, neglect, or harm that falls within the scope of the law,

Chapter 8

they are required to report it promptly to the appropriate authorities. Failure to report in such cases can lead to legal consequences for the individual who neglects this reporting obligation. Ultimately, a Christian's first phone call or meeting when realizing or expecting abuse should be to 911, the emergency telephone number for requesting assistance from fire departments, police departments, or medical services in urgent situations. Any attempt to become an investigator or to check out stories is illegal and, in my opinion, morally corrupt.

The main purpose of mandatory reporting is to ensure that timely intervention and protection measures are taken for those in danger. By requiring professionals and individuals to report such incidents, the hope is to prevent further harm and provide support and assistance to those in need.

Note that mandatory reporting is not intended to replace the role of law enforcement or child protection services but to complement their efforts in safeguarding vulnerable individuals. By fulfilling their reporting duties, mandated reporters play a critical role in protecting the welfare and well-being of those who may be at risk in their communities.

Read Romans 13. Read it again!

CHAPTER 9

Clear and Direct Communication

Effective counseling starts with the counselor being attentive and empathetic, taking the time to truly grasp the sufferers' circumstances and the impact it has had on them emotionally and spiritually.

It is vital that we as biblical counselors stay away from euphemisms and keep the counseling session moving forward. We must focus on clear and direct communication while relying on the guidance and principles from the Bible. Here are some strategies to achieve this:

- *Study Bible language.* Familiarize yourself with the terminology and style used in the Bible. This will help you communicate in a more straightforward and unambiguous manner, avoiding modern euphemisms that might lead to confusion or misinterpretation.

- *Choose precise words.* Instead of using euphemisms or vague language, opt for precise and specific words to convey your thoughts and messages. The Bible itself uses precise language to communicate God's teachings and wisdom.

- *Focus on biblical principles.* Ground your counseling approach in biblical principles and teachings, providing clear guidance and direction to the individual seeking counsel. The Bible offers profound insights that can address various life challenges and provide a solid foundation for counseling sessions.

- *Encourage openness and honesty.* Create an atmosphere of trust and openness where the individuals feel comfortable expressing their thoughts and emotions without the need for euphemisms. Emphasize the importance of honesty and vulnerability in the counseling process.

- *Engage in active listening.* Pay close attention to the person's words and emotions during the counseling session. Active listening allows you to understand the counselee's concerns fully and respond with appropriate biblical guidance, avoiding the use of ambiguous language.

- *Ask open-ended questions.* Encourage the person to elaborate on his or her feelings and experiences by asking questions that elicit more than a simple yes or no. This approach promotes deeper discussion and helps you address issues directly without the need for euphemisms.

- *Clarify misunderstandings.* If counselees use euphemisms or unclear language, kindly ask them to elaborate or provide more context. This will help you gain a clear understanding of their situation and respond more effectively.

- *Use biblical examples.* Refer to specific stories and people from the Bible that relate to the person's situation. These narratives often provide valuable insights and solutions without relying on euphemisms or vague language.

- *Pray for guidance.* Seek God's wisdom and guidance in your counseling sessions through prayer. Ask for clarity in communication and understanding, both for yourself and the person you are counseling.

- *Respect individual differences.* Recognize that each person may have a unique communication style and perspective. Be patient and understanding as you navigate the counseling process, ensuring that you remain sensitive to the counselee's needs and emotions.

By applying these principles and strategies, you can conduct a focused and fruitful biblical counseling interview while avoiding the use of euphemisms that might hinder clear communication and understanding.

CHAPTER 10

Recordkeeping

First and foremost, recordkeeping is an ethical responsibility that counselors must adhere to in order to protect the well-being of their counselees and maintain professional accountability. It allows counselors to accurately track the progress of the counseling relationship, assess the effectiveness of interventions, and make informed decisions about the course of treatment. By recording important details, such as the counselee's background, presenting issues, treatment goals, and the strategies used, counselors can ensure continuity of care and provide quality services.

What Records to Keep

Comprehensive recordkeeping involves a variety of elements including basic identifying information about the counselee, such as name, contact information, and relevant demographic details. It should also encompass a detailed history of the counselee's presenting problems, past experiences, and relevant family dynamics since these aspects can significantly impact the counseling process. Furthermore, documenting the goals and objectives set by both the counselor and the counselee helps to measure progress and evaluate the effectiveness of interventions.

Another crucial aspect of recordkeeping is the documentation of the counseling sessions. This includes a summary of the Bible verses and doctrines used, topics discussed, the strategies used, and the outcomes achieved during each session. It is essential to maintain accurate and objective notes, avoiding subjective interpretations that could bias future sessions or interventions. Additionally, any relevant assessments, tests, or tools used in the counseling process should be included in the records to provide a comprehensive picture of the counselee's progress.

It is recommended that all the following records be kept for every counselee:

1. **Basic Information:** Date, time, location, and duration of the session

2. **Client Information:** Name, contact details, relevant personal background, and any pertinent demographic information

3. **Presenting Issues:** Clear description of the counselee's concerns, reasons for seeking counseling, and any immediate issues discussed during the session

4. **Goals:** Collaboratively established objectives or goals for the counseling process, including desired short-term and long-term outcomes

5. **Assessment and Diagnosis:** Initial assessment of the counselee's mental, emotional, and/or relational functioning as well as any diagnostic impressions if applicable

6. **Bible Plan:** Detailed plan outlining the Bible verses and doctrines used, topics discussed, strategies used, and outcomes achieved during each session

7. **Progress Notes:** Summary of what occurred during the session, including topics discussed, interventions used, counselee responses, and any notable observations or insights

8. **Homework Assignments:** Any tasks or exercises assigned to counselees to complete between sessions to support their progress and growth, noting whether the homework was completed and turned in on time [Note: I only give one memory verse per week and sections of the Bible for reading. Using fill-in-the-blank handouts is essential. Ensure that the counselee is attending church weekly. I stop counseling if a counselee will not attend church.]

9. **Follow-up Plan:** Next steps or plans for future sessions, including scheduled follow-up appointments and any referrals or resources recommended [Note: I never meet more than once a week and aim to get to bi-weekly. More than three months of counseling is too long.]

10. **Confidentiality Statement:** Confirmation adherence to ethical guidelines and legal regulations regarding privacy and confidentiality

11. **Counselor's Reflections:** Personal reflections or insights from the counselor's perspective, including observations about the counselee's progress, challenges encountered, and areas for further exploration or development

12. **Informed Consent:** Documentation of the counselee's informed consent for counseling services, including understanding of the counseling process, goals, risks, and confidentiality policies

13. **Signature:** Signatures of both the counselor and the counselee to acknowledge the accuracy of and agreement with the contents of the counseling record

Maintaining accurate and thorough counseling records is essential for providing effective and ethical care, ensuring continuity of treatment, and promoting accountability and professionalism in the counseling process.

Benefits of Recordkeeping

Benefits of thorough recordkeeping extend beyond maintaining professional standards. It also ensures the protection of client confidentiality and privacy, as counselors can implement secure storage and access protocols for their records. Additionally, comprehensive records can be valuable in cases of potential legal or ethical issues, providing evidence of the counselor's adherence to professional guidelines and ethical standards.

For counselees, accurate recordkeeping enhances the quality of care they receive. It allows counselors to track their progress, identify patterns or recurring issues, and adjust interventions accordingly. Through transparent recordkeeping, counselees can actively participate in their treatment by reviewing the goals and strategies discussed during sessions.

Furthermore, well-maintained records provide continuity of care for counselees who may require counseling services in different settings or with different counselors. If a counselee moves or seeks services from another counselor, having access to comprehensive records can ensure a seamless transition and prevent the need to repeat previously discussed topics or assessments.

Guidelines for Recordkeeping

- *Computer Records:* All computer records must be securely password protected. Access should be limited solely to the counselor and those individuals specified in the counseling agreement. Confidentiality is paramount, and records should never be accessible to unauthorized individuals.

- *Hard Copy Records:* Hard copies of records should be kept under lock and key to ensure their safety and confidentiality. When it comes to inactive records, a standard practice is to dispose of them after a period of seven years.

- *Confidentiality:* Discussions regarding counselees or their situations should remain strictly confidential and confined to consulting professionals who are directly involved in the counseling process. Maintaining this confidentiality fosters trust and ensures the privacy of the counselees.

- *Homework Records:* Documentation of assigned homework or tasks given to counselees should also be maintained as part of the counseling process. This can provide valuable insights into the progress and efforts of the counselees.

By following these rules, counselors can effectively manage and protect the records of their counselees, ensuring that privacy is maintained and that counseling sessions are conducted with the utmost professionalism and ethical standards.

In conclusion, recordkeeping is an indispensable aspect of the counseling process. It not only demonstrates professional responsibility and adherence to ethical standards but also promotes continuity of care and client empowerment. By maintaining accurate and comprehensive records, counselors can effectively monitor progress, evaluate the effectiveness of interventions, and ensure that their counselees receive the best possible care. Moreover, thorough and accurate recordkeeping reinforces the trust and rapport between counselor and counselee, providing the foundation for a successful counseling journey.

APPENDIX A

Helping Hurting People Understand the Biblical Need for Military and First Responders to Kill

Over the past two decades, I've encountered a recurring question that weighs heavily on the minds of many individuals serving in our military and police forces. It typically manifests in this form: "During my time in the military, I was tasked with killing the enemy. While I'm not well-versed in the Bible, I'm aware of the commandment, 'Thou shalt not kill.' However, I've also come across biblical accounts depicting battles resulting in significant loss of life. Will God judge me unfavorably for having taken lives in combat? Is there hope for me to attain salvation?"

The Bible indeed presents what seems to be a contradiction at first glance. It unequivocally prohibits killing people, yet it also portrays numerous instances of killing and warfare. This apparent conflict arises from the intricacies of language and context within the biblical text.

In the sixth commandment, as stated in Exodus 20:13, the phrase "thou shalt not kill" is a translation from the Hebrew word ratsach. It's crucial to understand that Hebrew, like many languages, offers distinctions that point to different types of killing. Ratsach specifically denotes premeditated killing or what we might term as first-degree murder. It refers to the deliberate taking of a life, often driven by anger or malice, such as plotting and carrying out a murder in cold blood.

Some Bible scholars have pointed out that this type of killing doesn't refer to defending one's home from nighttime burglars (Exod 22:2), accidental killings (Deut 19:5), execution by the government (capital punishment) of those who have committed murder (Gen 9:6), or involvement in war—as when Israel went to war (Num 31:17, Josh 6:21). Interestingly, in Genesis 9:6, God told Noah after the flood that whoever kills a person must be killed (speaking of murder). The reason God gave for this law was that He had made humans in His image. Yet God gave this instruction right after the Flood—an event that wiped out everyone not in the ark. This is confusing, isn't it?

People in the military aren't the only professionals who have to wrestle with this issue. Law enforcement personnel deal with it too. Although police officers don't kill criminals nearly as often as is depicted on TV, there are times they might be faced with killing another human being. Does that mean we shouldn't have a police force? And should we not have a military? Most people accept the need for a military and a police force. Of course, they want a humane force rather than an aggressive one.

In the United States, prior to going to war, our leaders always look at the just war doctrine, which is a set of principles and criteria derived from moral and ethical considerations to guide a nation in determining the justification for conducting a war. While not an official doctrine codified in law, it draws on both religious (biblical reasons used for going to war) and philosophical traditions as well as international law to provide a framework for evaluating the morality of engaging in armed conflict. In other words, will fighting the enemy promote health and peace and stop useless killing? Essentially, is it fulfilling the Lord's command to kill a person who murders a person or people (Gen 9:6)?

In the American context, the principles of the just war doctrine typically include the following:

1. **Just Cause:** War must be waged for a morally defensible reason, such as self-defense against aggression, defense of innocent life, or the protection of basic human rights.

2. **Last Resort:** All peaceful alternatives must have been exhausted before resorting to war. Diplomatic negotiations, sanctions, and other nonviolent means should be pursued whenever possible.

3. **Legitimate Authority:** War must be declared by a competent authority, usually a legitimate government or international body, in accordance with established legal procedures.

4. **Right Intention:** The primary objective of going to war must be to establish a just peace rather than for selfish gain, revenge, or the destruction of the enemy.

5. **Proportionality:** The use of force must be proportional to the harm suffered or threatened, with the goal of minimizing civilian casualties and collateral damage.

6. **Probability of Success:** There must be a reasonable chance of achieving the war's objectives, and the benefits of victory must outweigh the costs and suffering involved.

7. **Noncombatant Immunity:** Civilians and noncombatants must be protected from intentional harm, and efforts should be made to avoid targeting them directly.

8. **Discrimination:** Combatants must distinguish between lawful military targets and noncombatants, and they should only attack legitimate military objectives.

Appendix A

The American just war doctrine seeks to balance the moral imperative to uphold justice and protect human dignity and life with the practical realities of international relations and the necessity of defending against aggression or injustice. It provides a moral framework for assessing the legitimacy of military action and guiding decisions about when and how to use force in pursuit of national security and global stability. Ultimately, it provides a biblical framework for keeping peace, health, and welfare.

To further understand the just war doctrine, we need to remember that in the Bible, there are numerous instances where the Lord is depicted as allowing or even commanding the killing of enemies. Some notable examples include these:

1. **Old Testament Battles:** Throughout the Old Testament, there are accounts of battles where God instructs the Israelites to fight against their enemies. For instance, in the conquest of Canaan, Joshua led the Israelites into battle against various Canaanite tribes with the understanding that it was God's will for them to possess the land (Josh 1–12).

2. **Divine Retribution:** In certain instances, God is portrayed as executing judgment on wicked nations or individuals through warfare. An example is the destruction of Sodom and Gomorrah (Gen 19), when God intervened directly to punish their wickedness.

3. **Warrior God Imagery:** In poetic passages, God is sometimes described in warrior-like terms, such as in Exodus 15:3, which says, "The LORD is a man of war: the LORD is his name."

4. **Military Leaders as Instruments of God:** Throughout Israel's history, military leaders such as Gideon, Deborah, and David are depicted as instruments of God's will in battles against enemy nations or oppressors.

It's important to note that these passages are clearly interpreted as a need and an order for a just war doctrine. Within the confines of biblical knowledge there is a time to kill.

In this world there is evil, and people mess things up, yet God is the one constant and is for life. Jesus said, "The thief cometh not, but for to steal, and to kill, and to destroy: I am come that they might have life, and that they might have it more abundantly" (John 10:10). Jesus also said, "Fear not them which kill the body, but are not able to kill the soul: but rather fear him which is able to destroy both soul and body in hell" (Matt 10:28). Each person must face death—both death on this planet and the possibility of an eternal death (or eternal life). Both matter. But strangely, in promoting life, sometimes you must kill. If a crazy man goes on a shooting spree, it might require shooting him so that he won't kill any more people.

In a war or civil disturbance, killing people is done to put an end to the killing/war. Indeed, killing to save life can be very strange. If you go into the military or become a police officer, you'll be trained to kill and to do it efficiently. You will take orders from a superior officer rather than making those kinds of decisions for yourself. The military doesn't work if each person decides for himself or herself what to do. You must obey orders. I applaud you for asking yourself these hard questions. Just remember that.God is for life. I am sorry some are ordered to kill, but know that your Lord was and is still beside you.

The following information has been compiled to aid in understanding the prerequisites for accepting Jesus Christ as your Lord and Savior according to the teachings of the Bible. Please read it attentively, and if needed, multiple times, to grasp the requirements outlined for salvation.

During my twenty-six years of military service, I often awaited my next orders. As a military professional, I was aware that orders from a higher headquarters could come at any time. The Bible teaches that life is no different! As a matter of fact, it states that your final orders are coming from heaven. Eventually, God will stop your breathing, and you will die. "It is appointed unto men once to die, but after this the judgment" (Heb 9:27). If you have not accepted the Lord Jesus as your Savior, your final orders will send you to hell for all eternity. The Lord states, "Whosoever was not found written in the book of life was cast into the lake of fire" (Rev 3:20). The good news is that "God hath not appointed us to wrath [punishment in hell], but to obtain salvation [eternity in heaven] by our Lord Jesus Christ" (1 Thess 5:9).

Knowing exactly where your next assignment will take you is a dream come true! Your final assignment in life will be determined by the decision you make after reading this information. If you want to choose hell as your final assignment, do nothing! You have already done enough! "The wicked shall be turned into hell" (Ps 9:17). If you desire heaven to be your final assignment, there are several steps you must take.

First, you must understand that you are a sinner. The Bible states, "For all have sinned, and come short of the glory of God" (Rom 3:23). All people are sinners and thus do not deserve to go to heaven.

Secondly, you must realize that your sin has deadly consequences. The Bible says, "The wages of sin is death" (Rom 6:23). Here, death refers to an eternal separation from God in hell.

Thirdly, you need to recognize that your sin debt has been paid. The Bible states, "God commendeth his love toward us, in that, while we were yet sinners, Christ died for us" (Rom 5:8). Jesus Christ, the Son of God, took your punishment and died for you!

Fourthly, you must repent of your sins. "God . . . now commandeth all men every where to repent" (Acts 17:30). Repentance is a change of heart that causes you to turn toward God and away from your present way of life.

Finally, you must take action to ensure that higher headquarters knows your intentions. "If thou shalt confess with thy mouth the Lord Jesus, and shalt believe in thine heart that God hath raised him from the dead, thou shalt be saved. For with the heart man believeth unto righteousness; and with the mouth confession is made unto salvation" (Rom 10:9–10). This passage lists two aspects of salvation. You are required both to ask Jesus to save you and also to believe God's Word. If you ask for salvation but do not believe with your heart, you are still on your way to hell.

To become a Christian, you must believe God's promises and act on them by asking Him to save you. God cannot lie! Here is His promise to you: "He that believeth on the Son hath everlasting life: and he that believeth not the Son shall not see life; but the wrath of God abideth on him" (John 3:36). If you will accept Jesus Christ as your Savior, please pray this prayer or one similar to it: "Lord Jesus, I admit I am a sinner, going to hell. I know that I cannot save myself. I repent of my sins and put my faith in the blood that You shed for me on the cross to pay for all my sins. I now accept You as my Savior and trust You to take me to heaven. Thank You for saving me. Amen."

APPENDIX B

Replacing Sinful Behavior with Godly Behavior

PUT OFF AND PUT ON (EPHESIANS 4:22–32)

Appendix B

PUT OFF	SCRIPTURE	PUT ON
ADULTERY	**Matthew 5:27–28** Ye have heard that it was said by them of old time, Thou shalt not commit adultery: But I say unto you, That whosoever looketh on a woman to lust after her hath committed adultery with her already in his heart. **Exodus 20:14** Thou shalt not commit adultery.	FIDELITY
ANGER	**Proverbs 14:17** He that is soon angry dealeth foolishly: and a man of wicked devices is hated. **Galatians 5:24–25** And they that are Christ's have crucified the flesh with the affections and lusts. If we live in the Spirit, let us also walk in the Spirit.	SELF-CONTROL
BAD LANGUAGE	**Ephesians 4:29** Let no corrupt communication proceed out of your mouth, but that which is good to the use of edifying, that it may minister grace unto the hearers. **1 Timothy 4:12** Let no man despise thy youth; but be thou an example of the believers, in word, in conversation, in charity, in spirit, in faith, in purity.	EDIFYING SPEECH
BAD MOTIVES	**1 Samuel 16:7** But the LORD said unto Samuel, Look not on his countenance, or on the height of his stature; because I have refused him: for the Lord seeth not as man seeth; for man looketh on the outward appearance, but the Lord looketh on the heart. **Psalm 19:14** Let the words of my mouth, and the meditation of my heart, be acceptable in thy sight, O LORD, my strength, and my redeemer. **Proverbs 23:7** For as he thinketh in his heart, so is he: Eat and drink, saith he to thee; but his heart is not with thee. **Proverbs 21:2** Every way of a man is right in his own eyes: but the LORD pondereth the hearts.	PURE MOTIVES FROM MEDITATING ON GOD
BITTERNESS	**Hebrews 12:15** Looking diligently lest any man fail of the grace of God; lest any root of bitterness springing up trouble you, and thereby many be defiled. **Colossians 3:12** Put on therefore, as the elect of God, holy and beloved, bowels of mercies, kindness, humbleness of mind, meekness, longsuffering.	TENDER-HEARTED-NESS
BOASTING	**1 Corinthians 4:7** For who maketh thee to differ from another? and what hast thou that thou didst not receive? now if thou didst receive it, why dost thou glory, as if thou hadst not received it? **Proverbs 27:2** Let another man praise thee, and not thine own mouth; a stranger, and not thine own lips.	HUMILITY
BODILY HARM	**Proverbs 16:29** A violent man enticeth his neighbour, and leadeth him into the way that is not good. **1 Thessalonians 2:7** But we were gentle among you, even as a nurse cherisheth her children.	GENTLENESS

Replacing Sinful Behavior with Godly Behavior

PUT OFF	SCRIPTURE	PUT ON
BURYING TALENTS	**Luke 12:48** But he that knew not, and did commit things worthy of stripes, shall be beaten with few stripes. For unto whomsoever much is given, of him shall be much required: and to whom men have committed much, of him they will ask the more.	PERFECTING ABILITIES
CHEATING	**Proverbs 15:3** The eyes of the Lord are in every place, beholding the evil and the good. **Luke 8:15** But that on the good ground are they, which in an honest and good heart, having heard the word, keep it, and bring forth fruit with patience.	HONESTY
COMPLACENCY	**James 4:17** Therefore to him that knoweth to do good, and doeth it not, to him it is sin. **Colossians 3:23** And whatsoever ye do, do it heartily, as to the Lord, and not unto men.	DILIGENCE
COMPLAINING	**Jude 1:15-16** [The Lord comes] to execute judgment upon all, and to convince all that are ungodly among them of all their ungodly deeds which they have ungodly committed, and of all their hard speeches which ungodly sinners have spoken against him. These are murmurers, complainers, walking after their own lusts; and their mouth speaketh great swelling words, having men's persons in admiration because of advantage. **Hebrews 13:5** Let your conversation be without covetousness; and be content with such things as ye have: for he hath said, I will never leave thee, nor forsake thee.	CONTENTMENT
CONDUCT IN CHURCH	**Hebrews 10:25** Not forsaking the assembling of ourselves together, as the manner of some is; but exhorting one another: and so much the more, as ye see the day approaching. **Ecclesiastes 5:1** Keep thy foot when thou goest to the house of God, and be more ready to hear, than to give the sacrifice of fools: for they consider not that they do evil.	REVERENCE
"COPPING OUT"	**II Timothy 1:7** For God hath not given us the spirit of fear; but of power, and of love, and of a sound mind. **Luke 14:27** And whosoever doth not bear his cross, and come after me, cannot be my disciple.	SELF-DISCIPLINE
COVETOUSNESS	**Exodus 20:17** Thou shalt not covet thy neighbour's house, thou shalt not covet thy neighbour's wife, nor his manservant, nor his maidservant, nor his ox, nor his ass, nor any thing that is thy neighbour's. **Colossians 3:5** Mortify therefore your members which are upon the earth; fornication, uncleanness, inordinate affection, evil concupiscence, and covetousness, which is idolatry.	YIELDING RIGHTS

Appendix B

PUT OFF	SCRIPTURE	PUT ON
CROWD-PLEASING	**Mark 8:36** For what shall it profit a man, if he shall gain the whole world, and lose his own soul? **Matthew 6:33** But seek ye first the kingdom of God, and his righteousness; and all these things shall be added unto you.	FOLLOWING JESUS CHRIST
DANCING	**1 Thessalonians 5:22** Abstain from all appearance of evil. **1 Corinthians 10:31** Whether therefore ye eat, or drink, or whatsoever ye do, do all to the glory of God.	GLORIFYING GOD
DATING PEOPLE IN LESS THAN GOD-HONORING RELATIONSHIPS	**2 Corinthians 6:14** Be ye not unequally yoked together with unbelievers: for what fellowship hath righteousness with unrighteousness? and what communion hath light with darkness? **1 Corinthians 6:12** All things are lawful unto me, but all things are not expedient: all things are lawful for me, but I will not be brought under the power of any.	BEING EQUALLY YOKED
DISCONTENTMENT	**Philippians 4:11–13** Not that I speak in respect of want: for I have learned, in whatsoever state I am, therewith to be content. I know both how to be abased, and I know how to abound: every where and in all things I am instructed both to be full and to be hungry, both to abound and to suffer need. I can do all things through Christ which strengtheneth me. **Hebrews 13:5** Let your conversation be without covetousness; and be content with such things as ye have: for he hath said, I will never leave thee, nor forsake thee.	SATISFACTION
DISOBEDIENCE	**1 Samuel 12:15** But if ye will not obey the voice of the Lord, but rebel against the commandment of the Lord, then shall the hand of the Lord be against you, as it was against your fathers. **Hebrews 5:9** And being made perfect, he became the author of eternal salvation unto all them that obey him.	OBEDIENCE
DOUBT OR UNBELIEF	**1 Thessalonians 5:24** Faithful is he that calleth you, who also will do it. **Hebrews 11:1** Now faith is the substance of things hoped for, the evidence of things not seen.	FAITH
DRINKING	**Proverbs 23:20** Be not among winebibbers; among riotous eaters of flesh. **Proverbs 23:29–33** Who hath woe? who hath sorrow? Who hath contentions? who hath babbling? Who hath wounds without cause? Who hath redness of eyes? They that tarry long at the wine; They that go to seek mixed wine. Look not thou upon the wine when it is red, When it giveth his colour in the cup, When it moveth itself aright. At the last it biteth like a serpent, And stingeth like an adder. Thine eyes shall behold strange women, And thine heart shall utter perverse things.	TREATING THE BODY AS GOD'S TEMPLE

Replacing Sinful Behavior with Godly Behavior

PUT OFF	SCRIPTURE	PUT ON
DRUG ABUSE	**Revelation 21:8** But the fearful, and unbelieving, and the abominable, and murderers, and whoremongers, and sorcerers, and idolaters, and all liars, shall have their part in the lake which burneth with fire and brimstone: which is the second death. **1 Corinthians 3:16–17** Know ye not that ye are the temple of God, and that the Spirit of God dwelleth in you? If any man defile the temple of God, him shall God destroy; for the temple of God is holy, which temple ye are.	TREATING THE BODY AS GOD'S TEMPLE
EVIL THOUGHTS	**Proverbs 23:7** For as he thinketh in his heart, so is he: Eat and drink, saith he to thee; But his heart is not with thee. **Philippians 4:8** Finally, brethren, whatsoever things are true, whatsoever things are honest, whatsoever things are just, whatsoever things are pure, whatsoever things are lovely, whatsoever things are of good report; if there be any virtue, and if there be any praise, think on these things.	THINKING ON PURE THINGS
FORNICATION	**1 Thessalonians 4:3–7** For this is the will of God, even your sanctification, that ye should abstain from fornication: that every one of you should know how to possess his vessel in sanctification and honour; not in the lust of concupiscence, even as the Gentiles which know not God: that no man go beyond and defraud his brother in any matter: because that the Lord is the avenger of all such, as we also have forewarned you and testified. For God hath not called us unto uncleanness, but unto holiness. **1 Corinthians 10:8** Neither let us commit fornication, as some of them committed, and fell in one day three and twenty thousand.	PURITY
GOSSIPING	**1 Timothy 5:13** And withal they learn to be idle, wandering about from house to house; and not only idle, but tattlers also and busybodies, speaking things which they ought not. **Romans 14:19** Let us therefore follow after the things which make for peace, and things wherewith one may edify another.	SPEAKING TO EDIFY
HATRED	**Matthew 5:21–22** Ye have heard that it was said by them of old time, Thou shalt not kill; and whosoever shall kill shall be in danger of the judgment: but I say unto you, That whosoever is angry with his brother without a cause shall be in danger of the judgment: and whosoever shall say to his brother, Raca, shall be in danger of the council: but whosoever shall say, Thou fool, shall be in danger of hell fire. **1 Corinthians 13:3** And though I bestow all my goods to feed the poor, and though I give my body to be burned, and have not charity, it profiteth me nothing.	LOVE OR KINDNESS

Appendix B

PUT OFF	SCRIPTURE	PUT ON
HOMOSEXUAL BEHAVIOR	**Romans 1:26–27** For this cause God gave them up unto vile affections: for even their women did change the natural use into that which is against nature: and likewise also the men, leaving the natural use of the woman, burned in their lust one toward another; men with men working that which is unseemly, and receiving in themselves that recompence of their error which was meet. **1 Timothy 5:22** Lay hands suddenly on no man, neither be partaker of other men's sins: keep thyself pure.	LIVING OUT GOD'S PURPOSE
HYPOCRISY	**Job 8:13** So are the paths of all that forget God; and the hypocrite's hope shall perish. **Ephesians 4:25** Wherefore putting away lying, speak every man truth with his neighbour: for we are members one of another.	HONESTY
IDLE WORDS	**Matthew 12:36** But I say unto you, That every idle word that men shall speak, they shall give account thereof in the day of judgment. **Proverbs 21:23** Whoso keepeth his mouth and his tongue keepeth his soul from troubles.	BRIDLED TONGUE
IMMODESTY	**Proverbs 11:22** As a jewel of gold in a swine's snout, so is a fair woman which is without discretion. **I Timothy 2:9-10** In like manner also, that women adorn themselves in modest apparel, with shamefacedness and sobriety; not with broided hair, or gold, or pearls, or costly array; But (which becometh women professing godliness) with good works.	MODESTY *This pertains to men as well.
IMPATIENCE	**James 1:2–4** My brethren, count it all joy when ye fall into divers temptations; Knowing this, that the trying of your faith worketh patience. But let patience have her perfect work, that ye may be perfect and entire, wanting nothing. **Luke 21:19** In your patience possess ye your souls.	PATIENCE
IMPROPER RELATIONSHIPS	**1 Corinthians 15:33** Be not deceived: evil communications corrupt good manners. **Philippians 1:20** According to my earnest expectation and my hope, that in nothing I shall be ashamed, but that with all boldness, as always, so now also Christ shall be magnified in my body, whether it be by life, or by death.	GOD'S STANDARDS
INHOSPITABLENESS	**1 Peter 4:9** Use hospitality one to another without grudging. **Romans 12:10, 13** Be kindly affectioned one to another with brotherly love . . . distributing to the necessity of saints; given to hospitality.	HOSPITALITY

Replacing Sinful Behavior with Godly Behavior

PUT OFF	SCRIPTURE	PUT ON
IRRITATION WITH OTHERS	**Proverbs 25:8** Go not forth hastily to strive, lest thou know not what to do in the end thereof, when thy neighbour hath put thee to shame. **Philippians 2:3-4** Let nothing be done through strife or vainglory; but in lowliness of mind let each esteem other better than themselves. Look not every man on his own things, but every man also on the things of others.	ESTEEMING OTHERS IN LOVE
JEALOUSY	**Proverbs 27:4** Wrath is cruel, and anger is outrageous; but who is able to stand before envy? **1 Corinthians 13:4** Charity suffereth long, and is kind; charity envieth not; charity vaunteth not itself, is not puffed up.	TRUST OR PREFERRING ONE ANOTHER
JUDGMENT-ALISM	**Matthew 7:1-2** Judge not, that ye be not judged. For with what judgment ye judge, ye shall be judged: and with what measure ye mete, it shall be measured to you again. **John 8:9** And they which heard it, being convicted by their own conscience, went out one by one, beginning at the eldest, even unto the last: and Jesus was left alone, and the woman standing in the midst.	SELF-EXAMINATION
LACK OF LOVE	**1 John 4:7-8, 20** Beloved, let us love one another: for love is of God; and every one that loveth is born of God, and knoweth God. He that loveth not knoweth not God; for God is love. . . . If a man say, I love God, and hateth his brother, he is a liar: for he that loveth not his brother whom he hath seen, how can he love God whom he hath not seen? **John 15:12** This is my commandment, That ye love one another, as I have loved you.	LOVE
LACK OF MODERATION	**Philippians 4:5** Let your moderation be known unto all men. The Lord is at hand. **2 Peter 1:5-9** And beside this, giving all diligence, add to your faith virtue; and to virtue knowledge; and to knowledge temperance; and to temperance patience; and to patience godliness; and to godliness brotherly kindness; and to brotherly kindness charity. For if these things be in you, and abound, they make you that ye shall neither be barren nor unfruitful in the knowledge of our Lord Jesus Christ. But he that lacketh these things is blind, and cannot see afar off, and hath forgotten that he was purged from his old sins.	BALANCE IN LIFE
LACK OF JOY	**Philippians 4:4** Rejoice in the Lord alway: and again I say, Rejoice. **1 Thessalonians 5:16** Rejoice evermore.	REJOICING ALWAYS

Appendix B

PUT OFF	SCRIPTURE	PUT ON
INSUBMISSION AND DISRESPECT	**2 Timothy 3:6** For of this sort are they which creep into houses, and lead captive silly women laden with sins, led away with divers lusts. **Matthew 6:10** Thy kingdom come. Thy will be done in earth, as it is in heaven.	BROKEN WILL
LAZINESS	**Ephesians 5:15–16** See then that ye walk circumspectly, not as fools, but as wise, Redeeming the time, because the days are evil. **Proverbs 6:6–11** Go to the ant, thou sluggard; consider her ways, and be wise: which having no guide, overseer, or ruler, provideth her meat in the summer, and gathereth her food in the harvest. How long wilt thou sleep, O sluggard? When wilt thou arise out of thy sleep? Yet a little sleep, a little slumber, a little folding of the hands to sleep: so shall thy poverty come as one that travelleth, and thy want as an armed man.	DILLIGENCE
LOSING ONE'S TEMPER	**Proverbs 16:32** He that is slow to anger is better than the mighty; and he that ruleth his spirit than he that taketh a city. **Romans 5:3–4** And not only so, but we glory in tribulations also: knowing that tribulation worketh patience; and patience, experience; and experience, hope.	SELF-CONTROL
LOSING ONE'S FIRST LOVE	**Revelation 2:4** Nevertheless I have somewhat against thee, because thou hast left thy first love. **1 John 4:10, 19** Herein is love, not that we loved God, but that he loved us, and sent his Son to be the propitiation for our sins. . . . We love him, because he first loved us.	MEDITATION ON CHRIST
LUST OF THE EYES	**1 John 2:16** For all that is in the world, the lust of the flesh, and the lust of the eyes, and the pride of life, is not of the Father, but is of the world. **James 1:14–15** But every man is tempted, when he is drawn away of his own lust, and enticed. Then when lust hath conceived, it bringeth forth sin: and sin, when it is finished, bringeth forth death.	PURE THOUGHTS
LUST OF THE FLESH	**1 John 2:16** For all that is in the world, the lust of the flesh, and the lust of the eyes, and the pride of life, is not of the Father, but is of the world. **1 Peter 2:11** Dearly beloved, I beseech you as strangers and pilgrims, abstain from fleshly lusts, which war against the soul.	PURE DESIRES

Replacing Sinful Behavior with Godly Behavior

PUT OFF	SCRIPTURE	PUT ON
LYING	**Ephesians 4:25** Wherefore putting away lying, speak every man truth with his neighbour: for we are members one of another. **Zechariah 8:16** These are the things that ye shall do; speak ye every man the truth to his neighbour; execute the judgment of truth and peace in your gates.	SPEAKING TRUTH
MURDER	**Exodus 20:13** Thou shalt not kill. **Romans 13:10** Love worketh no ill to his neighbour: therefore love is the fulfilling of the law.	LOVE OR KINDNESS
MURMURING	**Proverbs 19:3** The foolishness of man perverteth his way: and his heart fretteth against the Lord. **1 Corinthians 10:10** Neither murmur ye, as some of them also murmured, and were destroyed of the destroyer.	GRATEFUL-NESS
NECKING OR PETTING	**1 Corinthians 7:1** Now concerning the things whereof ye wrote unto me: It is good for a man not to touch a woman. **1 Thessalonians 4:4** Every one of you should know how to possess his vessel in sanctification and honour.	ABSTINENCE
NEGLECTING BIBLE STUDY	**2 Timothy 3:14–17** But continue thou in the things which thou hast learned and hast been assured of, knowing of whom thou hast learned them; and that from a child thou hast known the holy scriptures, which are able to make thee wise unto salvation through faith which is in Christ Jesus. All scripture is given by inspiration of God, and is profitable for doctrine, for reproof, for correction, for instruction in righteousness: that the man of God may be perfect, throughly furnished unto all good works. **Psalm 119:9–11** Wherewithal shall a young man cleanse his way? By taking heed thereto according to thy word. With my whole heart have I sought thee: O let me not wander from thy commandments. Thy word have I hid in mine heart, that I might not sin against thee.	FAITHFUL TO DEVOTIONS
NEGLECT OF PRAYER	**1 Thessalonians 5:17** Pray without ceasing. **Psalm 55:17** Evening, and morning, and at noon, will I pray, and cry aloud: and he shall hear my voice.	PRAYING
NO SOUL-WINNING DESIRE	**Proverbs 11:30** The fruit of the righteous is a tree of life; and he that winneth souls is wise.	SOUL-WINNING

Appendix B

PUT OFF	SCRIPTURE	PUT ON
SELFISHNESS/ NOT TITHING	**Malachi 3:10** Bring ye all the tithes into the storehouse, that there may be meat in mine house, and prove me now herewith, saith the Lord of hosts, if I will not open you the windows of heaven, and pour you out a blessing, that there shall not be room enough to receive it. **2 Corinthians 9:6–7** But this I say, He which soweth sparingly shall reap also sparingly; and he which soweth bountifully shall reap also bountifully. Every man according as he purposeth in his heart, so let him give; not grudgingly, or of necessity: for God loveth a cheerful giver.	GIVING/ TITHING
NOT DOING YOUR BEST	**Ecclesiastes 9:10** Whatsoever thy hand findeth to do, do it with thy might; for there is no work, nor device, nor knowledge, nor wisdom, in the grave, whither thou goest. **Colossians 3:23** And whatsoever ye do, do it heartily, as to the Lord, and not unto men.	DOING YOUR BEST
WORSHIPING FALSE GODS	**Deuteronomy 11:16** Take heed to yourselves, that your heart be not deceived, and ye turn aside, and serve other gods, and worship them. **Ephesians 4:6** [There is] one God and Father of all, who is above all, and through all, and in you all.	WORSHIPPING THE ONE TRUE GOD
OVEREATING	**1 Corinthians 9:27** But I keep under my body, and bring it into subjection: lest that by any means, when I have preached to others, I myself should be a castaway.	SELF-CONTROL
FAVORITISM	**James 2:1–6** My brethren, have not the faith of our Lord Jesus Christ, the Lord of glory, with respect of persons. For if there come unto your assembly a man with a gold ring, in goodly apparel, and there come in also a poor man in vile raiment; and ye have respect to him that weareth the gay clothing, and say unto him, Sit thou here in a good place; and say to the poor, Stand thou there, or sit here under my footstool: are ye not then partial in yourselves, and are become judges of evil thoughts? Hearken, my beloved brethren, Hath not God chosen the poor of this world rich in faith, and heirs of the kingdom which he hath promised to them that love him? But ye have despised the poor. Do not rich men oppress you, and draw you before the judgment seats? **Luke 6:31** And as ye would that men should do to you, do ye also to them likewise.	FAIRNESS
PRESUMING ON THE FUTURE	**James 4:13–14** Go to now, ye that say, To day or to morrow we will go into such a city, and continue there a year, and buy and sell, and get gain: whereas ye know not what shall be on the morrow. For what is your life? It is even a vapour, that appeareth for a little time, and then vanisheth away. **Proverbs 27:1** Boast not thyself of to morrow; For thou knowest not what a day may bring forth.	HAVING PATIENCE

Replacing Sinful Behavior with Godly Behavior

PUT OFF	SCRIPTURE	PUT ON
PRIDE	**Proverbs 16:18** Pride goeth before destruction, and an haughty spirit before a fall. **James 4:6** But he giveth more grace. Wherefore he saith, God resisteth the proud, but giveth grace unto the humble.	HUMILITY
PROCRASTI-NATION	**Proverbs 6:6-8** Go to the ant, thou sluggard; consider her ways, and be wise: Which having no guide, overseer, or ruler, Provideth her meat in the summer, and gathereth her food in the harvest.	PUNCTUAL-ITY
PROFANITY	**Psalm 109:17** As he loved cursing, so let it come unto him: as he delighted not in blessing, so let it be far from him. **1 Timothy 4:12** Let no man despise thy youth; but be thou an example of the believers, in word, in conversation, in charity, in spirit, in faith, in purity.	EDIFYING WORDS
REBELLION	**1 Samuel 15:23** For rebellion is as the sin of witchcraft, and stubbornness is as iniquity and idolatry. **Joel 2:12-13** Therefore also now, saith the LORD, turn ye even to me with all your heart, and with fasting, and with weeping, and with mourning: and rend your heart, and not your garments, and turn unto the LORD your God: for he is gracious and merciful, slow to anger, and of great kindness, and repenteth him of the evil.	SUBMISSION TO THE LORD JESUS
SASSING OR BACK TALKING	**John 6:43** Jesus therefore answered and said unto them, Murmur not among yourselves. **Ephesians 5:18-19** Be filled with the Spirit; speaking to yourselves in psalms and hymns and spiritual songs, singing and making melody in your heart to the Lord.	RESPECTING AUTHORITY
SELFISHNESS	**Philippians 2:21** For all seek their own, not the things which are Jesus Christ's. **John 12:24** Verily, verily, I say unto you, Except a corn of wheat fall into the ground and die, it abideth alone: but if it die, it bringeth forth much fruit.	DEATH TO SELF
SMOKING	**1 Corinthians 3:16-20** Know ye not that ye are the temple of God, and that the Spirit of God dwelleth in you? If any man defile the temple of God, him shall God destroy; for the temple of God is holy, which temple ye are. Let no man deceive himself. If any man among you seemeth to be wise in this world, let him become a fool, that he may be wise. For the wisdom of this world is foolishness with God. For it is written, He taketh the wise in their own craftiness. And again, The Lord knoweth the thoughts of the wise, that they are vain.	TREATING THE BODY AS GOD'S TEMPLE

Appendix B

PUT OFF	SCRIPTURE	PUT ON
SPEEDING	**1 Peter 2:13–14** Submit yourselves to every ordinance of man for the Lord's sake: whether it be to the king, as supreme; or unto governors, as unto them that are sent by him for the punishment of evildoers, and for the praise of them that do well.	OBEYING TRAFFIC LAWS
STEALING	**Ephesians 4:28** Let him that stole steal no more: but rather let him labour, working with his hands the thing which is good, that he may have to give to him that needeth. **Luke 6:38** Give, and it shall be given unto you; good measure, pressed down, and shaken together, and running over, shall men give into your bosom. For with the same measure that ye mete withal it shall be measured to you again.	GIVING
STRIFE	**James 3:16** For where envying and strife is, there is confusion and every evil work. **Luke 6:31** And as ye would that men should do to you, do ye also to them likewise.	ESTEEM FOR OTHERS
STUBBORN-NESS	**1 Samuel 15:23** For rebellion is as the sin of witchcraft, and stubbornness is as iniquity and idolatry. **Romans 6:13** Neither yield ye your members as instruments of unrighteousness unto sin: but yield yourselves unto God, as those that are alive from the dead, and your members as instruments of righteousness unto God.	SUBMISSION
STUMBLING BLOCK	**1 Corinthians 8:9–11** But take heed lest by any means this liberty of yours become a stumblingblock to them that are weak. For if any man see thee which hast knowledge sit at meat in the idol's temple, shall not the conscience of him which is weak be emboldened to eat those things which are offered to idols; and through thy knowledge shall the weak brother perish, for whom Christ died? **Romans 14:21** It is good neither to eat flesh, nor to drink wine, nor any thing whereby thy brother stumbleth, or is offended, or is made weak.	STEPPING-STONE
TEMPORAL VALUES	**Matthew 6:19** Lay not up for yourselves treasures upon earth, where moth and rust doth corrupt, and where thieves break through and steal. **2 Timothy 2:4** No man that warreth entangleth himself with the affairs of this life; that he may please him who hath chosen him to be a soldier.	ETERNAL VALUES
UNFAITHFUL-NESS	**1 Corinthians 4:2** Moreover it is required in stewards, that a man be found faithful. **Psalm 31:23** O love the LORD, all ye his saints: for the Lord preserveth the faithful, and plentifully rewardeth the proud doer.	FAITHFUL-NESS

Replacing Sinful Behavior with Godly Behavior

PUT OFF	SCRIPTURE	PUT ON
UNFORGIVING SPIRIT	**Mark 11:26** But if ye do not forgive, neither will your Father which is in heaven forgive your trespasses. **Matthew 6:14** For if ye forgive men their trespasses, your heavenly Father will also forgive you.	FORGIVING SPIRIT
UNGRATEFUL-NESS	**Romans 1:21** Because that, when they knew God, they glorified him not as God, neither were thankful; but became vain in their imaginations, and their foolish heart was darkened. **Ephesians 5:18, 20** Be filled with the Spirit; . . . giving thanks always for all things unto God and the Father in the name of our Lord Jesus Christ.	THANKFUL-NESS
WITCHCRAFT OR ASTROLOGY	**Deuteronomy 18:10** There shall not be found among you any one that maketh his son or his daughter to pass through the fire, or that useth divination, or an observer of times, or an enchanter, or a witch. **Micah 5:12** And I will cut off witchcrafts out of thine hand; and thou shalt have no more soothsayers.	WORSHIP OF THE ONE TRUE GOD
WORLDLY MUSIC	**Proverbs 23:7** For as he thinketh in his heart, so is he: Eat and drink, saith he to thee; but his heart is not with thee. **Ephesians 5:18–19** Be filled with the Spirit; speaking to yourselves in psalms and hymns and spiritual songs, singing and making melody in your heart to the Lord.	GODLY MUSIC
WORRY OR FEAR	**Ephesians 5:18–19** Be filled with the Spirit; speaking to yourselves in psalms and hymns and spiritual songs, singing and making melody in your heart to the Lord. **1 Peter 5:6–7** Humble yourselves . . . casting all your care upon him; for he careth for you.	TRUST OR FAITH
WRATH OR ANGER	**James 1:19** Wherefore, my beloved brethren, let every man be swift to hear, slow to speak, slow to wrath. **Galatians 5:24–25** And they that are Christ's have crucified the flesh with the affections and lusts. If we live in the Spirit, let us also walk in the Spirit.	SELF-CONTROL

APPENDIX C

Case Studies and Examples

The following are some practical examples and case studies illustrating the application of biblical counseling principles.

Chronic Pain

Situation: Ron suffers from perpetual excessive pain, and he feels suicidal. He hates going through his pain. He comes to your church and tells you that the pain is over the top, and he thinks that he would just be better off killing himself.

Responses: Ascertain if the pain is injury-related or PTSD. If it's from an injury, recommend Ron see a doctor. If it's PTSD, lead him to find refuge in the Lord (Ps 91:34, Rom 8:18, Rev 21:4.) Help him understand that life experiences and growth can often be painful (Matt 16:24, Rom 5:5). Suggest that God will give him purpose in life through helping others. Ultimately, make sure that he knows Christ as his Savior.

Come up with a plan of action that includes expectations and goals. It will be necessary to identify what Ron needs in order to determine what course of action to take. See if there's a way to get him into a support system with others who have similar issues. Other important questions to ask Ron include the following: What is your support system? What is your current relationship with God? What are you involved in as far as enjoyment goes? What is your aim in life? Do you desire to get better, or are you stuck in a rut?

Pray with Ron, and listen to him to make sure that you have all the information. Don't act like you relate to his pain if you don't. Remind Ron that God understands pain and suffering and that He didn't even exempt Himself from it. It was through pain and agony that the greatest victory (salvation) was won. Give scriptures. Follow God's pattern to help Ron use his own pain to bring about victories for others. Make sure that you follow up with Ron (James 1:2)

Anxiety and Depression

Situation: Jill suffers so badly from fear and worry that she hasn't left her house in a long time. She's living on disability and having her groceries delivered. She agrees to let you come over and counsel her.

Responses: Go to Jill's house, but do not go alone. Let her know that having that kind of stress and anxiety hurts physically and could be fatal. Inform her of the physical side effects of her depression and choosing to be housebound. Try to find out what her life was like before she became a reclusive person. Determine what caused her to start to withdraw from the world. Listen to her own diagnosis of the problem because you want her to see and be honest about what her problems are. If she doesn't acknowledge the problem, you can't help her change.

Formulate a treatment plan. As a counselor, realize that this is going to be a commitment. If it took Jill a long time to get here, it will take time for her to come out of it. Love her for who she is, not for what you're trying to do for her (e.g., thinking "I will fix this person"). Use Scripture to encourage her to resist her fear (Ps 91:2) and trust God (1 Pet 5:1). Philippians 4: 6–8 is a good passage to share with her. Encourage her to get out and take small steps. Pick her up and take her to church. Take her to buy groceries. Build slowly.

Emotional Numbness

Situation: John is emotionally numb. He has just started coming to church, so you don't know anything about him.

Responses: First, find out what his story is. This can start out as small talk so as not to push too hard. Build a relationship. This could take some time. Be patient. Over time, you may become comfortable enough to bring up salvation and spiritual matters. Gently encourage him to get involved with others (small social events or a support group) so that he can reconnect with his emotions. Give him some Bible verses that can be a comfort (e.g., 1 Pet 5:10, Rom 5:2–5, Isa 61:3, Heb 4:15). The counselor needs to understand that this relationship will take time and trust. Give John a purpose, something to do.

Repression

Situation: Bill doesn't want to share something. His wife says that he went through something that he doesn't want to talk about. Because of these traumatic events, he has withdrawn and isolated himself from others.

Responses: Talk to Bill and find out what the story is. Do what you can to get him involved in small groups and social activities; be sure to include his wife as well. Since the domino effect that PTSD has on family members can be quite extensive, she may need a support group or at least a listening ear as well. It's important that her needs be met just as his are so that the marriage can remain healthy, which will give them both some additional support. Proceed slowly with small, incremental steps. If you push too hard, Bill may retreat even more. Give Bill a purpose at home, at church, and at work. Remind him that life goes on and that he still has responsibilities (1 Cor 12:14, 1 Pet 2:23, 3:1–2, Eph 5, Col 3:16–24, Matt 5:13–14, 2 Cor. 1:4). This doesn't mean you should tell him to "just get over it," but that you encourage him not to quit.

Anger and Depression

Situation: Joan is always angry, anxious and on edge. She suffers from depression.

Responses: Build a relationship with her. Get her background story and get to know who she is. She is not her disorder, so be sure to separate the two and don't treat her as someone who needs to be "fixed." Don't minimize her issues. Find out if she is saved and what her relationship with God is like. Pay attention to how she's coping with her struggles, but don't jump to the conclusion that she's suicidal or harming herself (because making such an assumption can damage the relationship). Look for the warning signs, but don't ask her directly if she has plans to harm herself unless you have a reason to. Give her Bible verses on prayer and trust in God to help her change her thinking (Phil 4:6–8). Give her hope (Rom 5:3–5, 1 Kings 19, Ruth 1–4). Help her realize the possibilities of the future.

Unbelieving Spouse

Situation: Victor comes to your church, but his wife is an atheist and never attends. She suffers with PTSD.

Responses: Make sure Victor is saved and living the Christian life in front of his wife for her to see (1 Cor 7:16). Pray with Victor that God would work in his wife through him (Prov 21:1, John 16:7). Arrange a time to speak with Victor's wife, but don't necessarily push for this too soon. Be patient and make sure you have the right timing. (Ps 19:1–6, Rom 1:20, Isa 13:9-10, Acts 24:24)

Suicidal Thoughts

Situation: Suzie is a wife and mother and a member of the church, but she admits that she is suicidal and always considering suicide.

Responses: See if she has someone else to talk to about her struggle. If she is actively suicidal (i.e., has attempted to kill herself or has a plan to do so), she may need to be put on suicide watch. Walk her through the following points: (1) "You will have to give an account to God at the judgment." (2) "Consider the things in your future that you will miss if you end your life." You may want to share from 1 Kings 19 about Elijah's depression and thoughts of how it would be better to not be here, noting how God spoke to him and used him mightily.

Sexual Abuse

Situation: Johnny was raped and beaten when he was five years old, and now he struggles with emotional numbness among other things. He is saved, but he comes to you looking for additional help.

Responses: Check to see what Johnny's spiritual life is like. Reemphasize that he is a new creature in Christ (2 Cor 5:17) and that he is clean (1 John 1:7–9). Help him understand what real biblical love looks like (1 John 4:8, Rom 8:16). Build trust between him and yourself and maybe some others who are good listeners and genuinely care. Make sure you give him a purpose and a reason to overcome the depression and the hurt (e.g., so that he can use his experiences to help others).

Situation: Billie Jo was raped as a young girl, and she now suffers from emotional numbness and low self-esteem.

Responses: Be very careful to note that Billie Jo bears no blame for what happened to her and that it is normal to struggle after something so awful and it is not something to be ashamed of. Through Scripture, help her understand her own self-worth (Rom 8:15, 23, Eph 1:6, 2 Cor 1:4). Reassure her that God loves her and that He can use her experiences to help others struggling with something similar. Be sure she knows that she is not alone. Refer her to a qualified woman for further counseling.

Post-Traumatic Stress Disorder

Situation: James struggles with PTSD and refuses to leave his home.

Responses: First, talk to James to determine if he is saved and what his spiritual condition is. Get the background story if James is willing to share. If not, ask if there is someone else he would be willing to talk to (maybe a close friend or a therapist). Try to build a relationship with him yourself. Gently introduce him to activities outside of the home, including small-group social settings. Perhaps encourage him to have some people over to his house, bringing the social life to him until he is ready to venture outside his four walls. Give him a sense of purpose to improve and keep moving forward.

Situation: Sam, a former Navy SEAL, is married to one of the members in your church, but he refuses to come to church. His wife says that he is depressed.

Responses: Pray for Sam. People often say that prayer is the least they can do, but sometimes it's also the most they can do. It's a direct line to an all-powerful God, and that access to His power is not to be underestimated. Since PTSD can deeply impact the family as well as the individual, ask Sam's wife how she is doing. Is she staying strong in her Christian walk? Does she have anyone to talk to? Does she take care of herself by making sure that her personal/spiritual/emotional needs are met? Is she living out her Christian faith in such a way that her husband can see it?

Meet with Sam and try to find ways to connect with him (hobbies/likes/dislikes) so you can build a relationship. If you aren't the best person to do this, maybe you can connect him with someone has been through something similar. Be sure not to pretend to understand if you've never experienced anything like what he's gone through. Show grace; be loving and kind; listen! (Rom 5:20, 1 Cor 15, Phil 4:6–7).

APPENDIX D

Checklist for a Counseling Session

☐ Utilizing your questionnaire, fill in the blanks by gathering more data.

☐ If this is a second or later counseling session, review homework and goals to ensure completeness and a biblical understanding.

☐ Work throughout the counseling session on building rapport and a solid relationship.

☐ Determine ministry needs, i.e. what verses and biblical precepts must be covered?

☐ Assign homework with a goal sheet explaining what is expected.

☐ Review notes to determine if a mandatory report must be made.

Check off when each step is complete.

APPENDIX E

Pre-counseling Questionnaire

SAMPLE

HAMPTON ROADS BIBLICAL COUNSELING
A Ministry of Tabernacle Baptist Church
CONFIDENTIAL COUNSELING QUESTIONNAIRE

PERSONAL INFORMATION:
Name: _____ Today's Date: _____
Home Address: _____ City: _____ Zip _____
Phone Numbers: Work: _____ Home: _____ Cell: _____ E-mail: _____
How may we contact you (home/work, mail/phone, etc.)? _____
Gender: _____ Date of Birth: _____ Age: _____ Referred to us by: _____
Occupation: _____ Employer: _____
Education (yrs. completed): _____ Diplomas/Degrees: _____
Other Training (list type and years): _____
What are the name and ages of your siblings? _____
What is your birth order in your family of origin? _____

SPIRITUAL BACKGROUND:
Are you a member of a church? _____ If so, name: _____
Do you consider yourself a religious person? _____ Do you pray to God? _____
Do you read your Bible? _____ Do you believe in God? _____
Are you saved? _____ Please describe your experience. _____

Have you received believer's baptism by immersion? _____
Do you have regular individual devotions? _____
Do you have regular family devotions? _____
What church services do you attend? _____
How do you serve the Lord? _____

What are your spiritual goals? _____

Give us any further information on your spiritual life that you would like us to know: _____

HEALTH INFORMATION:
Rate your overall physical health: Excellent___ Good___ Average___ Fair___ Poor___
Do you get adequate rest (8-10 hours of sleep every night)? _____
Do you have problems sleeping? _____ if so, please describe: _____
Do you eat a balanced diet (food types/three balanced meals)? _____
Do you have a routine, weekly schedule? _____
Do you suffer from any prolonged medical conditions (high blood pressure, etc.)? _____

Pre-counseling Questionnaire

What medications, if any, do you take, the dosage, and how often? _____
Have you ever used drugs for other than medical purposes? _____
Have you ever had hallucinations? _____ if so, please explain: _____

Have you ever had an emotional or mental breakdown? _____ if so, please explain _____
_____

Have you seen a Psychiatrist _____, Psychotherapist _____, Psychologist _____?
If so, how long did you see your Psychiatrist _____, Psychotherapist _____, Psychologist _____?
Have you ever been hospitalized for this condition? _____
What diagnosis was given by the Psychiatrist? _____
Psychotherapist: _____, Psychologist: _____
What were the results of your therapy? _____
_____

INFORMATION ABOUT YOUR SPOUSE:
Name: _____
Home Address: _____
Phone Numbers: Work: _____ Home: _____ Cell: _____ Pager: _____
Gender: _____ Date of Birth: _____ Age: _____ Referred by: _____

Occupation: _____ Employer: _____
Education (yrs. completed): _____ Diplomas/Degrees: _____
Other Training (list type and years): _____

Does your spouse support you coming for counseling? _____

Is your spouse willing to come for counseling? _____

What are the name and ages of your spouse's siblings? _____
What is your spouse's birth order in his/her family of origin? _____

INFORMATION ABOUT CHILDREN:

Marriage	Child's Name	Age	Sex	Living	Education	Marital Status
Ex. first	Wendy Smith	13	F	with us	high school	single

Appendix E

MARRIAGE BACKGROUND:
Current Marital Status: _____ Single _____ Married _____ Separated _____
Divorced _____ Widowed/Widower _____
Age when married to current spouse: Husband _____ Wife _____
Length of engagement: _____ Date of Marriage: _____
Number of previous marriage: _____
Are you and your spouse close with both sides of the family? _____
Have there been any recent deaths in your families? ___ If so, who? _____ When? ___
Have you ever been separated? _____ If so, how long? _____
Are you legally separated? _____ Have you consulted an attorney? _____
Has either of you filed for divorce? _____ If so, when: _____
Have you petitioned a court for domestic issues? _____
Have there been any incidents of spouse or child abuse? _____ if so, please describe: _____
_____
_____

PROBLEM INFORMATION:
1. What seems to be troubling you?

2. How long has this condition lasted?

3. What have you done about the problem?

4. What are your expectations in coming here?

5. What brings you here at this point in time?

6. Is there any other information we should know or you would like to share?

Pre-counseling Questionnaire

What time frames are you available for meeting with a Biblical Counselor?

Sunday   after AM service   after PM service
Monday _____
Tuesday _____
Wednesday _____
Thursday _____
Friday _____
Saturday _____

I (We) understand that all of the foregoing information will be kept in strictest confidence subject to the Counseling Agreement that I (we) will enter into with my (our) counselor. I (We) further understand that this information is given to aid my (our) counselor in providing godly, Biblical counsel to help me (us) with my (our) problems and issues. To the best of my (our) information, knowledge, and belief the foregoing information is accurate at the time of reporting.

_____   _____
Date   Signature

_____   _____
Date   Spouse's Signature